Mirkka Koisko

Adult Learners' Learning in a University Setting

Hilkka Roisko

Adult Learners' Learning in a University Setting

A Phenomenographic Study

VDM Verlag Dr. Müller

Impressum/Imprint (nur für Deutschland/ only for Germany)
Bibliografische Information der Deutschen Nationalbibliothek: Die Deutsche Nationalbibliothek verzeichnet diese Publikation in der Deutschen Nationalbibliografie; detaillierte bibliografische Daten sind im Internet über http://dnb.d-nb.de abrufbar.
Alle in diesem Buch genannten Marken und Produktnamen unterliegen warenzeichen-, markenoder patentrechtlichem Schutz bzw. sind Warenzeichen oder eingetragene Warenzeichen der jeweiligen Inhaber. Die Wiedergabe von Marken, Produktnamen, Gebrauchsnamen, Handelsnamen, Warenbezeichnungen u.s.w. in diesem Werk berechtigt auch ohne besondere Kennzeichnung nicht zu der Annahme, dass solche Namen im Sinne der Warenzeichen- und Markenschutzgesetzgebung als frei zu betrachten wären und daher von jedermann benutzt werden dürften.

Coverbild: www.purestockx.com

Verlag: VDM Verlag Dr. Müller Aktiengesellschaft & Co. KG
Dudweiler Landstr. 99, 66123 Saarbrücken, Deutschland
Telefon +49 681 9100-698, Telefax +49 681 9100-988, Email: info@vdm-verlag.de
Zugl.: Tampere, University of Tampere, Diss. 2007

Herstellung in Deutschland:
Schaltungsdienst Lange o.H.G., Berlin
Books on Demand GmbH, Norderstedt
Reha GmbH, Saarbrücken
Amazon Distribution GmbH, Leipzig
ISBN: 978-3-639-09758-0

Imprint (only for USA, GB)
Bibliographic information published by the Deutsche Nationalbibliothek: The Deutsche Nationalbibliothek lists this publication in the Deutsche Nationalbibliografie; detailed bibliographic data are available in the Internet at http://dnb.d-nb.de.
Any brand names and product names mentioned in this book are subject to trademark, brand or patent protection and are trademarks or registered trademarks of their respective holders. The use of brand names, product names, common names, trade names, product descriptions etc. even without a particular marking in this works is in no way to be construed to mean that such names may be regarded as unrestricted in respect of trademark and brand protection legislation and could thus be used by anyone.

Cover image: www.purestockx.com

Publisher:
VDM Verlag Dr. Müller Aktiengesellschaft & Co. KG
Dudweiler Landstr. 99, 66123 Saarbrücken, Germany
Phone +49 681 9100-698, Fax +49 681 9100-988, Email: info@vdm-publishing.com

Copyright © 2008 by the author and VDM Verlag Dr. Müller Aktiengesellschaft & Co. KG and licensors
All rights reserved. Saarbrücken 2008

Printed in the U.S.A.
Printed in the U.K. by (see last page)
ISBN: 978-3-639-09758-0

CONTENT

1	INTRODUCTION	5
	1.1 Rationale for the Research	5
	1.2 Contribution to Research and Practice	7
	1.3 Research Questions	8
	1.4 Key Concepts of the Research	9
	1.5 Outline of the Research Report	11
2	THE RESEARCH CONTEXT	13
	2.1 The Case of TUKEVA	13
	2.2 The Researcher's Position	16
3	PHILOSOPHICAL UNDERPINNINGS	18
	3.1 Ontological Issues	19
	3.2 Epistemological Issues	21
	3.3 Axiological Issues	24
	3.4 The Idea of Man	25
4	THEORETICAL UNDERPINNINGS	28
	4.1 Learning from the Phenomenographic Viewpoint	29
	4.1.1 The Structure of Organisation of Awareness	32
	4.1.2 Theory of Variation	45
	4.2 Comparison of Learning Perspectives	47
5	METHODOLOGICAL UNDERPINNINGS	51
	5.1 Determining the Research Approach	51
	5.1.1 Criteria for the Choice of Approach	52
	5.1.2 Comparison of Alternative Methods	54

	5.2	The Phenomenographic Research Approach 59
		5.2.1 The Object of the Phenomenographic Approach 61
		5.2.2 Outcomes of the Phenomenographic Approach.................................63
		5.2.3 Criticism of the Phenomenographic Approach..................................67
6	IMPLEMENTATION OF THE RESEARCH...70	
	6.1	Selection of Participants..70
	6.2	Methods of Data Collection 73
		6.2.1 Conducting Interviews 74
		6.2.2 Collecting Written Data 81
	6.3	Evaluation of the Data Gathering Procedures and the Data..........................83
	6.4	Data Analysis 91
		6.4.1 Preparations for Analysis 93
		6.4.2 Phases of Analysis 94
7	RESULTS: ADULT LEARNERS' WAYS OF EXPERIENCING LEARNING AND PHENOMENOGRAPHY AS A RESEARCH APPROACH 105	
	7.1	Categories of Description..106
	7.2	Cognitive Phases of Learning 109
		7.2.1 Aggregation of Knowledge 110
		7.2.2 Memorisation 112
		7.2.3 Transforming Knowledge into Meaning..115
		7.2.4 Changed Views of Reality 119
	7.3	Integration of Theory and Practice..122
		7.3.1 Importing Knowledge into One's Work 124
		7.3.2 Improving One's Performance...125
		7.3.3 Merging Theory and Practice...126
		7.3.4 Developing One's Work 127
	7.4	Self-Regulation of Learning..129
	7.5	Professional Growth and Development 134
	7.6	Phenomenography as a Research Approach 143
8	DISCUSSION AND CONCLUSIONS 148	
	8.1	Principal Findings 148
	8.2	Contribution to Research and Practice..154

	8.3	Implications for Research and Practice 156
		8.3.1 Implications for Research using Phenomenography 156
		8.3.2 Implications for Pedagogical Practices 157
	8.4	Recommendations for Further Research 159
9		EVALUATION OF THE RESEARCH 161
	9.1	Theories of Truth 162
		9.1.1 Validity of the Research 164
		9.1.2 Reliability of the Research 168
	9.2	Generalisation of the Research 172
	9.3	Ethics of the Research 173
REFERENCES 175

1 INTRODUCTION

1.1 Rationale for the Research

The present book is a phenomenographic study on adult learners' learning at a university. The research interest in the subject arose from a desire and need to develop adult learners' learning at university and also research methods for investigating that learning. Despite the developmental orientation of the research, its ultimate aim is to contribute to basic research concerning the learning of adults studying alongside their work, and methods of exploring that learning.

The research was prompted by the fact that more and more adults take degree-oriented university studies while working full-time. For instance, in the Research Centre for Vocational Education (RCVE) of Tampere University, in which this research was accomplished, all the learners, no matter whether under- or postgraduate, are studying alongside their work. Similarly, the TUKEVA students, the focus group of this research, pursue their studies while working full-time. Studying for a degree under such circumstances is somewhat different from the traditional study mode at a university. Here, the researcher's point of view is that we adult educators do not yet have enough knowledge and understanding of adult learners' learning, especially with future prospects in mind. Hence the subject of adult learners' learning deserves to be minutely scrutinised.

Having been involved for many years in adults' education at university I became concerned about the efficacy of adults' learning and consequently sought a fresh perspective on the matter. My specific intention was to find a kind of perspective which might be helpful in educating adult learners for a future that is constantly changing and therefore partly unknown. My endeavour was challenged, for example, by Kyrö (2004) asserting that when circumstances change in on-going transitions the role of education is to renew and support individuals and organisations for the unknown future. Like her, I took the view that this causes pressure to understand the dynamics of learning in new and different ways.

However, promoting the theory of a certain issue often calls for the simultaneous promotion of methodology and methods investigating the same issue; that is, theoretical advancement goes largely hand in hand with methodological advancement. Thus, when it comes to the research methodology and methods in the field of adult learners' education, they likewise need to advance.

Regarding the research area in question there has recently been a shift from a normative paradigm to an interpretive one (Bron 2005, 27-28). This paradigm change is based on an increasing sophistication, both theoretical and methodological, of interpretivist researchers the world over (Denzin & Lincoln 2005, xv). I think that researchers' responsibility is first and foremost to be acquainted with the novel methodological tendencies of his/her field of research and to play a part in their supplementary sophistication, as well.

The methodology concerning adults' learning is today more interpretative, biographical and explorative than earlier. Respectively the methods producing scientific knowledge make use of a process of discovery. The research in the field has changed from a macro perspective towards a micro level, where an adult learner is considered as a person who learns and takes responsibility for his/her learning. Based on the previous viewpoint, the emphasis in adult education research is today on the learner's perspective. (Bron 2005, 26-27.)

In line with the methodological shift discussed above, a promising way to combine a study on adults' learning and methods investigating that learning was found here from an integration of the ideas of learning of new phenomenography and a phenomenographic research approach. This research therefore theoretically and methodologically advocates a phenomenographic research approach to adult learners' learning at a university. It concentrates especially on understanding the dynamics of learning in a new and different way. At the heart of phenomenography lies an interest in describing the phenomena in the world as others experience them, and in revealing and describing the variation therein, especially in an educational context. (e.g. Marton & Booth 1997, 111; Huusko & Paloniemi 2006.)

Phenomenography is quite a new approach and has been used in education research for some 25 years. It has so far gained a reputation especially in Sweden, its country of origin, in Hong Kong, Australia and in the United Kingdom. As a research approach, it initially emerged from a strongly empirical base, rather than a theoretical or philosophical one. And, it is only recently that epistemological and ontological postulations, theoretical bases of learning and methodological requirements underlying the phenomenographic approach have been more noticeably advanced. (Åkerlind 2005a, 321.) These advancements have recently led to the creation of the Variation Theory of learning and anatomy of learner's awareness, with their associated implications for learning, pedagogical practices and research on learning (see e.g. Marton & Tsui 2004). This research takes advantage of those novel improvements of phenomenography.

1.2 Contribution to Research and Practice

The present research makes use of phenomenography both as a theoretical perspective on learning and as an empirical research methodology. Based on this, I present my research as an example of a complete phenomenographic study conducted in such a way that all relevant aspects of the research are undertaken from a phenomenographic perspective (see e.g. Bowden 2000, 10). Hence, it may be realistic to suggest here that both the findings by themselves and the method by which the findings are obtained will introduce novel contributions to the field of end users of the research such as pedagogues, educators and researchers dealing with adult learners in universities.

In the field of the present research - adult learners' degree oriented university education alongside working-life - there is hardly any of this kind of phenomenographic research. By contrast, most phenomenographic studies in university settings involve mainstream students (see e.g. Tynjälä 1997, 1999a) but not those whose studies are pursued while in full-time employment. Based on that shortcoming, it is my intention that this study will contribute to the research field it advocates.

Furthermore, my observation is that in many studies (at least within the national research context) applying phenomenography, it has been used as merely a method of analyses but not as a holistic research approach taking into consideration the special premises phenomenography implies. In addition, phenomenography has recently evolved but this development towards new phenomenography has in general, in my view, not yet been satisfyingly recognised when conducting research.

And finally, I hope with this research to be able to take a tiny step towards theoretical and methodological improvements with regard to university level adult learners' learning and education. My intention concurs well with the strategy of our research community (RCVE), which also postulates that the researchers within that community are greatly striving for the advancement of research methodology and methods.

1.3   Research Questions

The purpose of this research is to gain knowledge and understanding of adult learners' learning in university settings by investigating and describing learners' ways of experiencing their learning there. The research builds on the phenomenographic approach of educational research and focuses on investigating adult learners' learning from the perspective of the learners themselves (e.g. Marton 1986; Marton & Booth 1997; Marton & Tsui 2004).

In the light of the foregoing, it should be noted that the research addresses the learners' perceptions of their learning experiences and therefore does not even try to distinguish actual (real) learning from perceived learning. In other words, the phenomenon this research is interested in is adult learners' learning (the subject of the research), for which knowledge and understanding are sought through learners' ways of experiencing (unit and object of the research) their learning.

The research addresses the following three research questions:

1. What kind of variation is there in adult learners' ways of experiencing their learning at a university?
2. What kind of a holistic view can be constituted from adult learners' various ways of experiencing their learning at a university?
3. What kind of research approach is phenomenography in investigating adult learners' experiences of their learning at a university?

The research is a part of a larger TUKEVA research project. TUKEVA is an educational project of eight years standing, funded by the European Social Fund (ESF). The name TUKEVA is an acronym from Finnish words meaning research, development and training. TUKEVA aims to combine working experience and on-the-job learning with degree studies for adults. The students involved in TUKEVA typically pursue their degree studies while in full-time employment.

1.4 Key Concepts of the Research

In order to provide the reader with a necessary knowledge base of the key concepts the research builds on these are presented below. The description of the concepts is made in relation to the topic of the research and the research questions. Although phenomenography involves a great deal of concepts that are specific to just that certain research approach, they are, however, not yet defined here, but in terms of their respective occurrence in the text.

Adult learner is taken in this research to be a learner who has professional experience and pursues his/her degree-oriented university studies while in full-time employment.

Learning is a change in person–world relationship (Fazey & Marton 2002, 246); it is a qualitative change in the way that some phenomenon is experienced by the learner (Marton &

Booth 1997, 142). Consequently, learning has occurred when the learner exhibits a change in his/her way of experiencing the phenomenon in the world (Uljens 1996, 117.)

Experience is an internal relation between the individual and the phenomenon in the world (Linder & Marshall 2003, 273), in the sense that experience is that which relates the subject (experiencer) to the object (that being experienced) (Prosser 2005, 8). Experience is the totality of ways in which human beings either make or try to make sense of what they consciously (being aware) perceive (Jarvis 2004, 104).

A way of experiencing something is to be described in terms of human beings' structure of organisation of awareness in a particular moment (Marton & Booth 1997, 100). The way we experience something depends on what aspects we are aware of and can discern simultaneously (Runesson 2006, 397).

Variation refers to the phenomenographic assumption that whatever phenomenon a human being encounters, it is possible to identify a limited number of varying ways in which the phenomenon is experienced (e.g. Marton 1997, 97).

Various ways of experiencing something can be described in terms of differences in human beings' structure of organisation of awareness at a particular moment or moments (Marton & Booth 1997, 100).

University setting is an environment in which to study for a degree according to the official curriculum in a formal university programme.

Research approach is a combination of those philosophical, theoretical and methodological underpinnings a certain research is founded on.

Phenomenography is the research of the structure of a variation in the way a something is experienced by a human being. It is not a full description of his/her experience, but a description of the key differences in the ways of experiencing. It does not describe the variation in individual experience but the variation in the experience of individuals as a collective. (Prosser 2005, 7.)

1.5 Outline of the Research Report

The structure of this research report is outlined in what follows. Chapter 2 describes the context in which the research takes place. It also positions the researcher in the research context and the subject area of the research. Chapter 3 provides a review of those philosophical underpinnings a phenomenographic research is founded on and the requirements the researcher must take into account when doing such research. Chapter 4 outlines the theoretical underpinnings with respect to learning, however, paying particular attention to a phenomenographic view of learning. Chapter 5 deals with the methodological issues of the research. It thoroughly describes phenomenography as a research approach and in comparison with certain other research methods. The chapter is followed by Chapter 6 which presents a detailed depiction of the sampling strategies, data collection methods and protocols utilised in the data analysis. Chapter 7 presents the results of the research and simultaneously answers to the research questions. Chapter 8 summarises the major findings and discusses the contributions and implications of the research. The research report concludes with Chapter 9 evaluating the quality of the research and demonstrating how the scientific criteria of validity and reliability were adapted to ensure the knowledge claims of the research.

And finally, as the study is based on several decisions Figure 1 as a point of departure, elucidates the chain of argumentation of the decisions taken when conducting the research. The left column in the figure identifies the chapter in which the topic is addressed in detail.

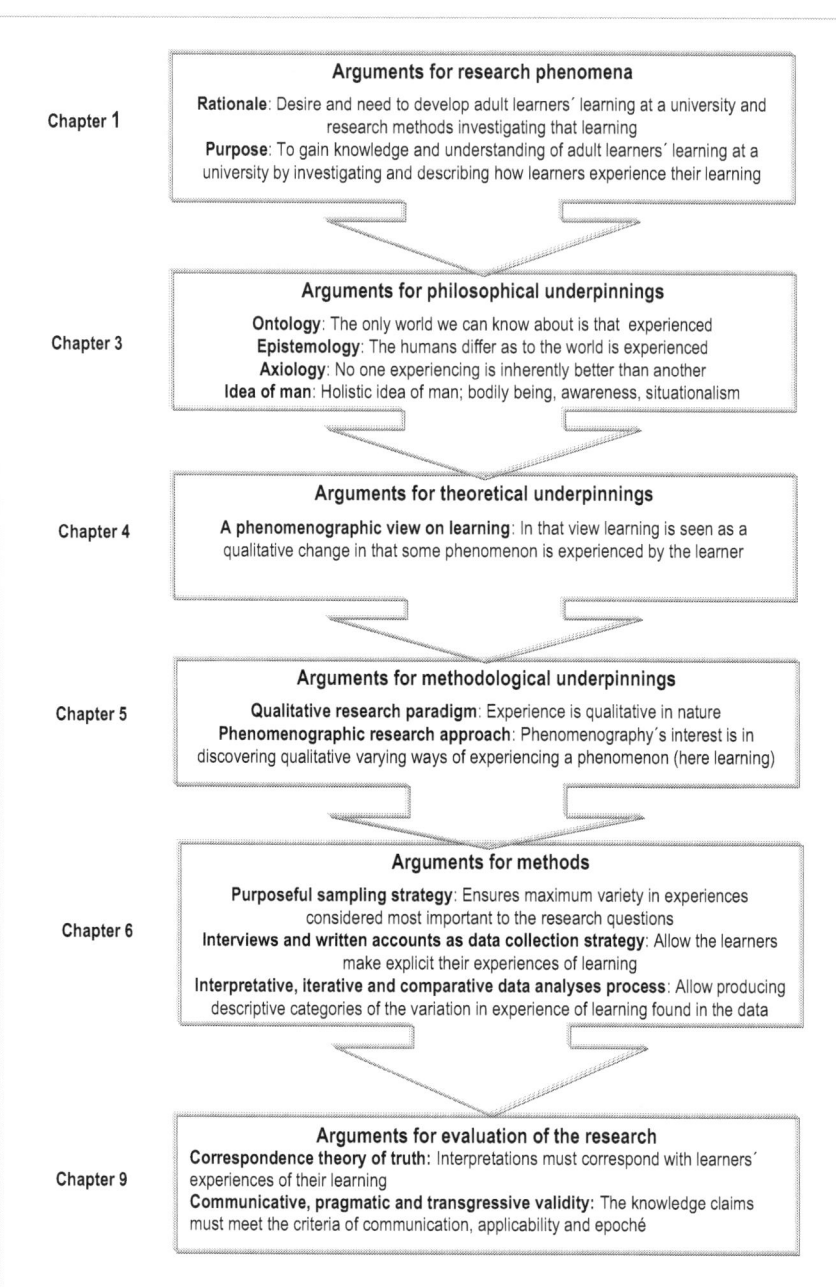

Figure 1. Chain of argumentation of decisions made in the research

2 THE RESEARCH CONTEXT

In the following, I present a comprehensive introduction to the case of TUKEVA, which forms the context for my research. This is intended to provide the reader with sufficient background knowledge of the research context, needed particularly when interpreting and evaluating my research. It is equally important for the reader to know the researcher's position in relation to the research context and the subject area of the research. Therefore also those matters are discussed at the end of the chapter.

2.1 The Case of TUKEVA

TUKEVA is a research, development and training project for vocational education; funded by the European Social Fund (ESF). The project started in 1998 and is due to end in 2006. TUKEVA's target groups are teachers and other staff at vocational training institutes, likewise their clients and partners in companies and municipalities. On a general level TUKEVA aims to give everyone involved an opportunity for learning and professional growth and to promote lifelong learning and educational effectiveness among adults.

In that kind of demanding educational endeavour research plays an enormously significant role by enhancing the understanding of learning and subsequently supporting those pedagogical decisions made when educating the TUKEVA students. For that reason there is an ongoing follow-up research on the quality and effectiveness of TUKEVA during the period 2002-2006. The initiative for the follow-up research came from me and I am also responsible for its implementation. As already mentioned in Chapter 1, the present study is a part of that larger TUKEVA follow-up research.

The core ideas of the TUKEVA project are to give teachers and other staff working on projects providing vocational training for adults, opportunities to update their knowledge and skills and simultaneously upgrade their academic status and degree. In doing this, TUKEVA also aims to combine working experience and on-the-job learning with degree studies for adults. The students involved are pursuing university degrees while in full-time employment. (Nieminen 2005.)

The other aims of TUKEVA include providing the universities and polytechnics with an opportunity to develop new forms of teaching and learning (for instance virtual learning environments) as well as to create cooperation and new networks between project partners. Disseminating information on vocational training and enhancing its status with the help of reports, publications and articles on the project are also included in TUKEVA's objectives. (ibid.)

In order to meet these requirements, TUKEVA supplies education and other forms of programmes in a flexible manner, taking into account the experience and skills those involved already have (ibid.), however, without jeopardising the curriculum goals of universities. TUKEVA is designed to acknowledge adults' experience and also to promote their self-directedness. Based on that, the study methods typically used are intensive lectures, project assignments, seminars and theses. Lectures usually take place at weekends, on Friday evenings and Saturdays, and are thus more appropriate for adult learners. Furthermore, the theses and project works are geared to be closely connected to the areas of the students' professional lives. The time needed for graduation depends on the level of the degree (bachelor, master, licentiate), and can on average be earned in three to six years.

The project started as a relatively flexible idea with national funding in 1998 and I was among the first to be recruited to co-ordinate the project. The first years were mainly used for planning, finding suitable partners and sufficient methods to fund the project. Within two years TUKEVA developed into a set of ESF-funded projects supported by several nationally financed sub-projects. The funding was provided by the Provincial State Offices of Finland, European Social Fund, Ministry of Education and the National Board of Education. (Nieminen 2005.)

The main partners, educators, disciplines and degrees in TUKEVA are: the Adult Education Co-ordination Unit (Aike Oy), which is responsible for the coordination of the whole TUKEVA project, and also the University of Jyväskylä (B.Sc. and M.Sc. (Econ.)); the University of Tampere (B.A. and M.A. (Educ.) and Lic.Educ.); the University of Oulu, coordination of technical education; Tampere University of Technology, Edutech (M.Sc. (Eng.)); Tampere University of Technology, Edupoint (M.Sc. (Eng.)); Helsinki University of Technology, Lahti Center (M.Sc. (Eng.)); Lappeenranta University of Technology (M.Sc. (Eng.)) plus several polytechnics and vocational teacher education units in Finland.

The degree targets in figures are 250 university degrees including tens of thousands of university points, and more than 500 vocational teachers as well as dozens of polytechnic degrees.

To summarise, TUKEVA pursues the development of all people and organisations involved by

- giving people opportunities to study flexibly at university and polytechnic level
- accepting people from various academic backgrounds to study on the programmes
- offering studies that both update knowledge and upgrade the academic standard of the participants
- making studying possible whilst working full-time
- combining studies directly with work
- giving students all this free of charge. (Nieminen 2005.)

So far TUKEVA's results seem to support the above goals very well. As Nieminen (ibid.) evaluates "Everything seems to indicate that the results aimed at can and will be achieved as planned and in some parts – exceeded".

2.2 The Researcher's Position

When doing qualitative research the researcher is not assumed to be a neutral mechanical data gatherer. Instead, he/she is seen as the main research instrument (e.g. Kvale 1996). It is conceded that his/her motivation, past history, positioning in the research context, and interactions with the research participants, all have an influence on the course of the research. This is considered unavoidable, and therefore, instead of trying to close her eyes to the matter the researcher should make her role and position explicit. (e.g. Case 2000, 94.) Hence, I next portray myself to give the reader an opportunity to understand my interest in and relationship to the present research. Information on my historical background is of great importance, particularly when justifying the quality of the research.

I have recently been working as a researcher in a follow-up research entitled The Quality and Effectiveness of the TUKEVA programme. This investigation is pursued under the responsibility of the Research Centre for Vocational Education (RCVE) at the University of Tampere. The research started in 2002 on my initiative. In addition to my researcher's duties, I coordinate some professional development courses intended for post-graduate students and supervise some undergraduates working on their first thesis at the university. I also take part in some additional tasks in our unit (RCVE), for instance, curriculum and quality assurance processes.

I am not a newcomer to the scene. I have my Master's degree (the thesis concerned self-directed learning of adults) and Licentiate's degree (the thesis concerned the meaning of learning for adults) in education, in which I have also gained extensive practical experience. In addition, I have qualifications in vocational teacher education and the competence of a work counsellor. Prior to starting my doctoral studies I worked over ten years in various positions (as a teacher, planning officer, coordinator, human-resource developer, manager of education, researcher) in the field of adult and vocational education at the Universities of Turku and Tampere as well as at the University of Applied Sciences (HAMK), and in the HAMK Vocational Teacher Education unit.

It is also worth mentioning that I was the one who set the TUKEVA programme in motion at the University of Tampere. I was responsible for the co-ordination of those studies in the Faculty of Education, in RCVE, for four years (1998 – 2002), that is, until the present research started. As a consequence of my previous position, I of course knew the TUKEVA programme very well, and was known to some of the students as well, especially to those studying at the University of Tampere.

The above biographical information largely explains my strong interest in the issues investigated in the present book.

3 PHILOSOPHICAL UNDERPINNINGS

When establishing knowledge about an aspect of reality, every research approach makes specific assumptions of its own about the nature of reality under investigation (ontology) and about the nature of knowledge (epistemology) (Sandberg 2005, 47). This research is based on a qualitative research paradigm and more specifically on the phenomenographic viewpoint. Phenomenography is here used in two different, but related, positions. On the one hand it forms a framework for the theory of learning used, and on the other hand it offers a solid methodological base for investigating that learning.

The researcher's loyalty to phenomenography, however, entails several commitments, among others, philosophical and methodological ones, which need to be considered when conducting this type of research. The philosophical underpinnings and their consequences are explained in this chapter in terms of ontology, epistemology, axiology, and the idea of man with respect to the current research. Ontology raises basic questions about the nature of reality (Guba and Lincoln 1994, 99, 105). It asks what the form and nature of reality are and what can be known about reality (Ponterotto 2005, 130). Epistemology, for one, asks how we know the world. What is the nature of the relationship between the knower and what can be known? (Guba & Lincoln 1994; 99, 105). And finally axiology concerns the role of the researcher's values in the scientific process (Ponterotto 2005, 131).

In phenomenography the ontological issue refers to the relation between a human being's awareness and reality, whereas the epistemological issue refers to the relation between theory and reality (Uljens 1996, 114). Awareness is the totality of a human being's experience (e.g. Rauhala 1995, 9). With regard to the axiological question the phenomenographers claim that the kind of learning they advocate is a powerful one, which gives rise to ethical implications (or that it builds on ethical commitments) (Bowden & Marton 2004, 208).

In elaborating the philosophical underpinnings of phenomenography, Marton (1994b) refers to the works of the phenomenologists Husserl (1859-1938) and Gurwitsch (1901-1973). According to this, there seems to be a relationship between phenomenography and phenomenological philosophy. This relationship has been developed and discussed in more detail, for example, by Theman (1983) Kroksmark (1987), Uljens (1996) and Sandberg (1994).

The discussion above aims to provide a general outline of the philosophical underpinnings to which my research is committed. What follows is a detailed description of those ontological, epistemological and axiological assumptions that supervised my challenging journey in the land of phenomenography. Finally, in the last section of the chapter I depict the nature of the human being (idea of man) as defined for the purposes of the present research.

3.1 Ontological Issues

It is claimed (e.g. Rauhala 1992; Perttula 1995) that before a researcher can posit and elaborate his/her hypothesis or decide upon his modes of approach, he/she must arrive at some preconception of the basic nature of his object. In other words, he must himself determine what his/her object of inquiry is, which means coming to an ontological decision.

The nature of the ontological analysis of research comes from the assumption that there exists an idea of the human being and the relationship between the human being and reality behind all research practices (see. e.g. Giorgi 2005). As mentioned in the previous section, the ontological issue in phenomenographic research refers to the relationship between awareness and reality (see Figure 2) (Uljens 1996, 114). Phenomenography represents a non-dualist position with respect to the ontological issue (e.g. Uljens 1996, 112-118; Marton & Booth 1997). Non-dualism is more commonly know as monism. In this research, however, I use the concept of non-dualism, as is customary in relation to phenomenography.

Non-dualist ontology claims that the human being is in an inseparable relation with reality (or some phenomenon in reality). Ramsden and Masters et al. (1993) capture that relationship aptly as they say that:

> ... there are not two worlds (an objective outside world and an internally constructed subjective world). There is only one world to which we have access - the world-as-experienced. (Ramsden et al. 1993, 303)

As becomes evident from the above quotation, the proponents of non-dualistic ontology assume that the only world we can know about (and consequently describe) is that which we experience. This entails that we cannot then sensibly talk about reality not experienced. What this implies is that humans' (here learners') different ways of experiencing the surrounding world are all there is. Therefore, in phenomenography, it is not possible to compare an individual's understanding with reality itself. (Uljens 1996, 112-113.)

Due to the non-dualistic point of view, the phenomenographers do not take the human being (the experiencer, e.g. the learner) and his/her reality (the experienced, e.g. learning) separately. On the contrary, they recognise that they are intertwined and argue that neither of them could be the way they are without the other (Bowden & Marton 2004, 206). To assume a dualist ontology is to treat subject and object as two separate entities and divide research object into two entities: a subject in itself and an object in itself (Sandberg 2005, 44).

The phenomenographers are not, however, saying that reality is just a construct of human beings (this point would be advocated by constructivists), but that reality is rather constituted through the reciprocally intertwined emergence of humans and their world (e.g. Prosser & Trigwell 1999, 13; Bowden & Marton 2004, 206-207). Furthermore, it is also assumed in phenomenography that everyone's reality (experience) reflects the world to the extent that it reflects us, constituting a part-whole relationship. And hence, the phenomenographers cannot imagine a world beyond the human being's experience. (Bowden & Marton 2004, 206-207.)

From the perspective of learning, and accordingly the present research, the non-dualistic view of phenomenography places emphasis on interpreting learners' perceptions of their own learning experiences at the centre (e.g. Prosser & Trigwell, 1999). This is because, as mentioned above, in phenomenographic reasoning the only phenomenon which will be described is the phenomenon as experienced by someone. Thus, there are, as noted by Sjöström and Dahgren (2002, 340), in a sense, several worlds to describe. That is, everyone has his/her own description.

The origin of the non-dualist position in phenomenography is, according to Uljens (1996, 112, referring to Marton 1992, 2), being specified against representational epistemology as well as dualistic ontology. Representational theories presuppose metaphysical dualism. That is, the existence consists of two different kinds of world (e.g. Saarinen 1994, 248), that constituted of objects and that constituted of a mental world. Hence, the phenomenographers are opposed to the idea that existence consists of two interrelated but ultimately independent realities: on the one hand a real world and one the other a representational world (Uljens 1996, 113; see also Marton & Booth 1997, 112-114).

3.2 Epistemological Issues

Epistemology refers primarily to three central questions for the researcher. First, how can individuals achieve meaning and thereby knowledge about the reality in which they live? Second, how is this knowledge constituted? Third, under what conditions can the knowledge achieved be claimed to be true? (Sandberg 2005, 47.) It is fundamental to understanding of the phenomenographic approach to realise that its epistemological stance is premised on intentionality, which affords a non-dualism and depicts experience as the internal relationship between human and the world, as noted by Pang (1999, 1). The idea of intentionality implies, in general, that individuals' awareness is not closed but dynamic and always directed toward something other than itself (discussed in more detail in Section 4.1.1) (Sandberg 2005, 48). Uljens (1996, 114) stipulates that even if a phenomenographer agrees to a non-dualist position, he/she must clarify the epistemological assumptions beyond his or her research, that is, how knowledge develops and how new knowledge is reached. As mentioned previously, the epistemological issue in phenomenography refers to the relationship between theory (language) and reality (Figure 2) (Uljens 1996, 114).

Prosser and Trigwell (1999, 13) propose that owing to the non-dualistic approach to experience, phenomenography is grounded in a constitutionalist epistemology. The essence of this view is that meaning is constituted through an internal relationship between the individual and the world. This idea is contrary to objectivist epistemology, which stipulates that beyond human awareness there is an objective reality. Thus, the qualities and the meaning of our experiencing are assumed to be inherent in reality itself. (Sandberg 2005, 44.)

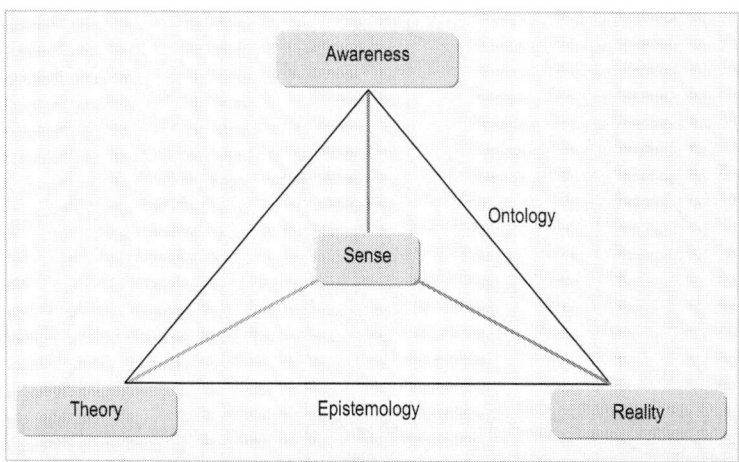

Figure 2. The relationship between the ontological and epistemological issues in phenomenography (adapted from Uljens 1996, 115)

The figure 2 above illustrates how ontological and epistemological concerns are related in phenomenography. In the figure, theory refers to the reality (epistemological concern) by means of awareness noting that theory has no direct access to a phenomenon (reality) but is always dependent on awareness and sense-making. In other words, theory is not a mirror of reality (see e.g. Giorgi 2002; Sandberg 2005). Therefore, awareness is primary in relation to theory (Uljens 1996, 114-115). Or, in Giorgi's (2002, 9) words "[p]erhaps there are things or events "in-themselves", but there is no "knowledge-in-itself". There is only knowledge for a human subject who apprehends it."

To sum up, phenomenography rests on a non-dualistic ontology, as the assumption is that because of the internal relationship between the human being and reality, the only world that we can communicate about is the world as experienced. The epistemological assumption, for one, is that humans differ as to how the world is experienced, but these differences can be described, communicated and understood by others. (Sjöström & Dahlgren 2002, 340.) Because of its non-dualistic stance, phenomenography takes a relational position (see e.g. Bowden & Marton 2004, 206) on knowledge. The present research takes accordingly the same position. Due to that the characteristics of relationality and relational knowledge are briefly discussed below.

The relational position on knowledge

According to Karvonen (1997) the principle of relationality means that neither we people nor other beings have an insulated, eternal, unchanging presence (essential). By virtue of this, in the relational viewpoint, the knowing subjects do not observe reality from the outside, but are inside the world, in the middle of it. Accordingly, the way the world appears to us depends on what we ourselves are and how we are related to the world. That is, linguistic descriptions, definitions, categories and meanings stem from our active interpreting of the relational realities of which we are a part. (ibid.)

The idea of relationality is contrary to realism, in which the human being is perceived as an external observer disconnected from the object of knowing. However, relationality does not mean a relativism in which knowledge becomes essentially a subjective matter of opinion. (ibid.)

Furthermore, following Karvonen's (ibid.) ideas, based on the relational point of view, knowledge is neither absolute nor objective or subjective, but it is based on a certain type of encounter, being in relation to the world. Thus knowledge is valid or invalid within a certain encounter and inside a certain setting into a relation, and its validity cannot necessarily be generalised to concern other kinds of relations.

Again, from the relational point of view, reality proves itself to us at every moment (see Section 4.1.1, Anatomy of Awareness). The starting point is not the relationship of knowing or observing the world but, on the contrary, our ontological, non-dualist being in relation to it. Therefore, the reality that we can experience or understand is relative, not absolute or original, reality. And we ourselves are parties in the formation of this relational reality. Thus, our understanding or knowledge is relational and limited, and our knowledge is also relative and produced inside some relation and, in that framework, valid and true. (ibid.)

3.3 Axiological Issues

This section of my work relates to the classical but ever essential question of what is good and what is right, which is an axiological problem. In connection with this research we should ask questions like: What kind of learning is good? Is there some learning that is not good? Who can judge good learning?

Such questions are much needed because phenomenographers argue for the particular view of learning they subscribe to being a powerful one (e.g. Bowden & Marton 2004, 208). However, they admit that such arguing entails important ethical implications, or that it builds on ethical commitments. Bowden and Marton decline to say that the good and the right are universally decreed, but claim that under certain circumstances good ethical principles go with the right yielding powerful learning. (ibid.)

With regard to the value of powerful learning Åkerlind (2002) has come a conclusion similar to that of Bowden and Marton (ibid.), when noting that while no single way of experiencing learning is inherently better than another, the inclusive nature of the relationships between the phenomenographic categories indicate that the categories higher in the hierarchy represent broader, more inclusive awareness of the various aspects of learning. And therefore, some views of learning will allow a greater flexibility than others in approaching one's learning under different contextual circumstances, as well as opportunity for engaging in more varied forms of learning. As a result of this, one would expect that views of learning in line with those higher in the hierarchy provide more powerful ways of learning. (ibid.)

From the point of view of the present research, I agree with the ideas that some ways of experiencing learning are under certain circumstances, for instance, in preparing learners for an unknown future, more effective and relevant than others. Yet, that stance does not imply being interested solely in that kind of learning. On the contrary, it necessitates taking all kinds of learning seriously in order to develop them even better.

3.4 The Idea of Man

Perttula (1995, 109) recommends that researchers commit themselves consciously to one assumption regarding idea of man and his/her relationship to reality and aim to make as logical conclusions about it as possible, which cover all the phases of the research project. However, it is important to understand that adopting a certain idea of man does not make one research approach realistic and other approaches, based on other ideas of man, unrealistic. Ontological analysis constructs the research on a justified but not necessarily a truthful basis. (ibid.)

According to Rauhala (1992, 32-33; 1993, 68) the idea of man includes the presuppositions and assumptions that the researchers of human behaviour have when they begin their work, or set their hypothesis and choose the appropriate methods to test them. The description of the idea of man should, therefore, be extensive enough to include all that is essential about a human being.

As noted previously, the philosophical roots of phenomenography are in phenomenology (see e.g. Uljens 1996). Hence, they share a common idea of man. From their viewpoint, human beings are creative and open meaning structures who experience and develop meanings and actualise as bodily, conscious personas in relation with their situation. The human persona is thus, on the one hand, a multi-dimensional, but, on the other hand, at the same time a holistic entity. (e.g. Rauhala 1992.)

The idea of man in this research is based on Rauhala's (e.g. 1981, 104; 1989, 27; 1992, 35) comprehensive, holistic idea of man. It perceives that people actualise in the following three basic modes of existence:

- bodily being (existence as an organic being)
- consciousness (the various qualities and degrees of experiences of existence)
- situationality (existence in relation to the life situation).

These three modes of man's existence are interdependent (Rauhala 1981, 104). Firstly, consciousness is realised (Rauhala 1989, 29-32; 1992, 37-38) when the mind (or meaningful content) (the Greek noema) becomes apparent in some phenomenon, object or matter. This realisation is about experiencing a sense or a sense being present in a realising way and affecting the people's existence. The basic structure of consciousness, the principle of noematicity (mindfulness), states that mind/sense appear and are proportionate through their meaning to each other. When the mind/sense relates to a phenomenon and means it (i.e. intention) human beings has a meaning relationship through which the object is understood as something. (ibid.)

Secondly, it has been claimed by Rauhala (ibid.) that situationality is equally essential part of the idea of man as bodily being and consciousness. By situationality is meant the inevitability of man's relationality to the world, situation being the term for the components of the world with which a given individual stands in relationship (Rauhala 1981, 104). According to Rauhala (1989, 32-39; 1992, 40-46), human beings are born, and they develop and are at all times in a relationship with their life situations. The life situation changes continuously because, for example, of education, working life, and the family communities that people belong to. When a change occurs in the life situation, the factual basis of which experiences get their content material also changes. When an experience changes new light is shed on the state of affairs of the situation. (ibid.)

Thirdly, experiences always occur with the help of the body. The body in its entirety offers the co-ordinates in which we experience something. In other words, we understand relations concerning space since we are spatial creatures, we experience time since we are realised in the rhythm of our vital functions and the historicity of our situation. In order to have experiences the body always has to have brains, in which the experience is realised. Thus, body is the condition for the existence of consciousness. (ibid.) Rauhala (1981, 105) comes to a conclusion, that for senseful meaning relationship to arise there must be a human individual in all his various modes of existence – situational, bodily and conscious.

To sum up, the adult learner is seen in this research as a human being who experiences, constitutes meanings and has a historical past (life world) of his/her own. This human being is multi-dimensional, and has his/her realisation in consciousness, bodily being and situationality, but existing at the same time as a holistic entity.

In the above I have presented an outline of the underlying ontological, epistemological and axiological assumptions of my research. I have also provided an illustration of the idea of man as it is seen from the perspective of this phenomenographic research. In keeping with the assumptions outlined above, the following chapter moves towards the theoretical underpinnings of the research.

4 THEORETICAL UNDERPINNINGS

In this chapter I will delineate the theoretical underpinnings of the study with respect to learning. Understanding learning is a complex undertaking dependent on a combination of several factors such as learner's background, learning environments and teaching practices. Consequently theories of learning provide different kinds of definitions of the word learning[1] as well as various explanations for how learning occurs.

While it is not the aim of this study to provide a detailed description of all learning theories, my intention is instead aimed at an adequate description particularly of the theory used, namely phenomenography. However, justifying the phenomenographic theory of learning for the purposes of the present study necessitates comparing it with some other predominant perspectives on learning, i.e. the constructivist perspectives. This is done in the last section of the chapter. For the moment I will focus on what is meant by the phenomenographic view of learning.

Since the phenomenographic theory of learning consists of several constituents, the dominant ones being anatomy of awareness and theory of variation, each of them will be discussed in separate sections. It should be noted, that the treatment of the issue of learning here is restricted to learning in formal[2] educational settings since that is the context in which this study is conducted.

---

[1] Illeris (2002, 14-15), for instance, discerns four different main meanings for the word learning. Firstly, the word learning can refer to the results of an individual learning process. Secondly, the word learning can refer to an individual psychological process. Thirdly, both learning and learning processes can refer to interaction processes between the individual and his or her material and social environment. Fourth, both learning and learning processes are used more or less simultaneously with the word teaching, which may be interpreted as what is taught and what is learned. The view of learning this phenomenographic research resembles the most, is the third.

[2] Formal is here taken as an antonym for informal. In connection with humans' learning, it is assumed (Wihlborg, year unknown) that two kinds of contexts are of importance. Firstly, one that corresponds to humans' common experiences and ongoing situations, which in teaching and learning situations are that of a formal context. Secondly, *one context which is that of informal character, which involves humans' individual experiences outside their situated* learning context.

4.1 Learning from the Phenomenographic Viewpoint

The theoretical framework adapted in this research is a theory of learning as presented by Marton and Booth (1997), Bowden and Marton (2004) and Marton et al. (2004). This theory rests on the phenomenographic research tradition. The origin of the tradition is to be found in empirical studies of learning among Swedish university students (e.g. Marton, 1974; Dahlgren, 1975; Säljö, 1975; Svensson, 1976).

Phenomenography was developed by a research group in the Department of Education at the University of Gothenburg in Sweden during the early 1970s. (Marton 1997, 95). The word "phenomenography" was coined in 1979 and it appeared for the first time in the work of Marton (1981) (Pang 2003, 145). Although the psychologist Ulrich Sonnemann already used the term "phenomenography" as early as in 1954, the impetus for the development of phenomenography did not occur until the 1970s (e.g. Hasselgren & Beach 1997). Etymologically, the term "phenomenography" derives from the Greek words "phainemenon" and "graphein". The combination of these two words makes phenomenography a description of appearances and is thus concerned about the description of things as they appear to human beings. (Pang 2003, 145-146.) Out of the empirical studies over about thirty years a theoretical and an analytical description of learning has been developed, i.e. a theory of variation and awareness.

Phenomenography is based on three assumptions regarding a human being's ways of experiencing the world around him/her. Firstly, phenomenographers believe that there are critical differences in human beings' ways of experiencing phenomena (in this study the phenomenon of learning). Secondly, phenomenographers suppose that different individuals can experience the same phenomenon differently, and thirdly the same individual can experience the same phenomenon differently. (e.g. Marton & Booth 1997.) Marton's (e.g. Marton 1997, 95) hypothesis, however, is that whatever phenomenon is taken into account, it can be understood in a limited number of different ways. Actually, Jarvis (2004, 94) states the same conclusion, "our consciousness of the world is not of the entire world, nor even the entire situation in which we find ourselves, since we actually focus on a single part of our externality".

The claim that individuals could understand a phenomenon in different ways is, according to Runesson and Marton (2000, 6), not unique to the phenomenographic research tradition (c.f. individual constructivism). However, what seem to be unique are its twofold aims; on the one hand to identify variation in experiencing the same phenomenon and on the other to identify differences in the variation that are critical for learning (ibid.).

While phenomenography subscribes to non-dualistic ontology (see Section 3.1), where the human being and reality are not seen as detached from each other, learning is understood as an internal relation between the learner and reality (e.g. Marton & Booth 1997; Marton & Fai 1999). In line with this, phenomenography defines learning as a change in the learner's capability to experience a phenomenon in the world (Marton & Booth 1997, 142; Marton & Fai 1999; Fazey & Marton 2002). The same idea is enviced by Uljens (1996, 117), who suggests that learning has occurred when an individual exhibits a change in his or her way of experiencing, seeing, perceiving the world. Marton and Booth (1997) characterise the kind of learning phenomenography advocates more precisely:

> The learning ...means that the learner has developed a capability to experience a certain phenomenon when it appears in a novel situation in a particular way (which goes beyond the other ways in which she has been capable of experiencing the phenomenon), which in turn means that the relationship between the learner and the phenomenon has changed. The learner has become capable of discerning aspects of the phenomenon other than those she had been capable of discerning before, and she has become capable of being simultaneously and focally aware of other aspects or more aspects of the phenomenon than was previously the case. (Marton & Booth 1997, 142)

When it comes to the effectiveness of phenomenographic learning, Marton et al. (2004, 8) assume that in relation to particular aims or objects of learning, some ways of experiencing are more powerful than others. Thus the way in which something is experienced by the learner is a fundamental feature of learning.

hierarchical nature of the categories in phenomenography as distinguishing the approach from grounded theory.

When contemplating the suitability of grounded theory for the present research, I came to the conclusion that it did not meet the requirements set for the method of this study. The main reason for this was its heavy emphasis on theory development. Although my aim was to focus on the phenomena of learning in a holistic way, my primary interest was not in theory formulation but in description and understanding. And further, like phenomenology, grounded theory also falls foul of accounting the idea that learners' experiences of their learning can be differentially distributed across learners, i.e. there is variation in learners' ways of experiencing learning.

To sum up the comparison of the methods thought to be adequate for the present research, the three different methods discussed above are placed side by side in Table 2. The depiction aims to argue for phenomenography as an appropriate approach for the purposes of the present study.

Learning as constitution

When speaking about learning the phenomenographers use such concepts as to constitute (a constitution) instead of, for example, to construct (a construction). In so doing, the proponents of phenomenography are assuming that reality is constituted through a reciprocal and intertwined emergence of human beings and their world (e.g. Bowden & Marton 2004, 206) and therefore subscribe to a constitutive view of learning. This point is clearly put by Marton and Booth:

> The world is not constructed by the learner, nor is it imposed upon her; it is constituted as an internal relation between them. (Marton and Booth 1997, 13)

Experience is seen as a constitutive potential that has a capacity to justify relationships between the human being and reality (learner and object of learning). This entails that the way in which human being experiences a phenomenon does not constitute the phenomenon itself but it rather constitutes one view of the phenomenon, seen from that human being's perspective, with his/her biography as a background. (Marton & Booth 1997, 124.) As further clarified by Anderberg (2000, 18), in constitutional thinking an experience is not regarded as a kind of introspective, mechanical, objectified procedure but as a constitutive, creative and reflective act.

According to phenomenography the learners do not find out about an independently constituted reality, on the contrary, they themselves participate in an ever ongoing constitution of that reality. This viewpoint is different from the thought that every learner constructs his/her own private reality, which is separate from the real world. And, it is likewise different from the idea that the learner grows into a world already constituted (cf. forward Section 4.2, discussing individual and social constructivism). Due to this, to experience reality is to participate in its constitution, although reality is more than one person can experience individually. (Marton 1996a, 176-177.) This is a view that is shared by other authors, for example by Rauhala (e.g. 2002), who also regarded constitution as a part of a human being's sense making.

As a consequence of the above discussed principles, in the constitutionalist perspective on learning the division between the external and internal worlds of the learner disappears. This means that the knower and the known, the subject and the object are not seen as separate (Marton & Booth 1997, 138) but through an internal relationship, as elaborated by Prosser and Trigwell:

> From a constitutionalist perspective on learning there is an internal relationship between the individual and the world. The individual and the world are not constituted independently of one another. Individuals and the world are internally related through the individuals' awareness of the world. The world is an experienced world. (Prosser & Trigwell 1999, 139)

To sum up, by assuming a constitutional perspective on learning the phenomenographers take a different attitude towards the knowledge and the existence of an objective world then, for example, the proponents of constructivism. In a phenomenographic line of reasoning knowledge is considered to exist in the relation constituted between an individual and the world (e.g. Cope 2004, 9-10).

4.1.1 The Structure of Organisation of Awareness

It is agreed by phenomenographers that there is a link between a human being's way of experiencing something and the structure of one's awareness[3]. Due to this, doing phenomenographic research means investigating the different ways in which human beings are aware of a certain phenomenon. From the point of view of the present research it denotes finding the differences in adult learners' structure of awareness with regard to their learning. Marton and Booth have stated this point:

> A way of experiencing something can thus be described in terms of the structure of organization of awareness in a particular moment. Similarly, qualitatively different ways of experiencing something can thus be described in terms of differences in the structure and organization of awareness at a particular moment or moments. (Marton & Booth 1997, 100)

While the issue of awareness lies at the heart of today's phenomenography it is described in detail in what follows. I first attempt to define the concept of awareness at a general level and

---

[3] *The anatomy of awareness constitutes a major theme of Marton and Booth's publication Learning and Awareness* (Marton & Booth 1997) where it is presented most thoroughly.

in relation to its adjacent concepts and thereafter proceed to elaborate its structural characters from a phenomenographic point of view.

On Defining Awareness

Here I agree with Rauhala (e.g. 1996, 35; 1998, 39), that a problem in research on consciousness and awareness is that people, including researchers, usually do not make a clear distinction between these two concepts but rather use them interchangeably. Marton and Booth (e.g. 1997, 99; 1998, 538) also accept using the terms "consciousness" and "awareness" synonymously, but themselves prefer the term "awareness" to maintain distance from the overwhelmingly dualistic use of consciousness. Greenfield (1999, 112), for instance, defines consciousness as "an emergent property of non-specialised groups of neurons...that are continuously variable with respect to an epicentre". Marton and Booth (1998, 538) elaborate the difference between the terms "consciousness" and "awareness" thinking of consciousness as being the opposite of unconsciousness and awareness as the opposite of lack of awareness. Uljens (1996, 106) draws a conclusion similar to Marton and Booth (ibid.) arguing that awareness (though referred to as consciousness) must be understood in terms of what a subject is aware of in being aware of something. In using these two concepts in this research I will side with the suggestions of Marton and Booth (ibid.) employing them as hierarchically differentiated constituents, adapted from Rauhala (e.g. 1998, 39 referring to Kaila, year unknown):

A. unconsciousness (noun), unconscious (adjective); (falls outside the interest of this research)
B. consciousness (noun), conscious (adjective); (falls within the interest of this research)
   - awareness (noun), aware (adjective); (falls within the particular interest of this research)
   - unawareness (noun), unaware (adjective); (falls outside the interest of this research)

Elaborating the hierarchical idea of the consciousness-awareness dimension above, some elucidations are needed. Regarding consciousness and awareness one should first exclude the existence of unconsciousness (Rauhala 1998, 37). That is because within unconsciousness it does not make sense to speak about aware (or unaware or lack of awareness) qualities of one's experience (ibid 42). Thereafter, consciousness in the whole of meanings is in this tangle of problems logically the primary matter. Aware (awareness) and unaware (unawareness) degrees of clarity can be divided only inside consciousness. Aware is a quality modifier that conveys the degree of clarity of contents or meanings. The content whose apparent existence in the clarity sector of consciousness cannot be sensibly denied is aware (comprising awareness). Unawareness cannot be sensibly included in awareness as the meaning of the division of the concepts above is in particular to show that unawareness is outside awareness. (Rauhala 1996, 35; 1997; 1998.)

Turunen (1998, 74), for one, illustrates consciousness as a special energy unity that is divided into numerous qualities: sensations, experiences, senses, feelings, images, thoughts and more. These kinds of qualities are the inside world of a human being beside the presumed outside or material world. According to this (ibid., 158) the existence of consciousness can be confirmed only from the perspective of awareness. In other words, consciousness exists only for awareness.

Awareness is a relation between subject and object (Marton 1997, 97), the totality of a person's simultaneous experiences and her relatedness to the world (Marton & Booth 1998, 538) at a given point in time (Marton & Booth 1997, 108). According to Rauhala (1998, 43) awareness is a subjective state, which is difficult to explain to another person. The clarity and sharpness of awareness are merely lived and experienced.

In the light of foregoing awareness is seen here as a sub-dimension of consciousness (which is the opposite of unconsciousness), and as the opposite of unawareness. It implies a human being's total experience of the world at a given point in time and of which the human being is aware. I will now continue by delineating the structure of awareness, as assumed in phenomenography. According to Rauhala (1995, 94), the question of the structure (anatomy) of awareness is above all a question of how do the meaning relationships organise themselves in one's awareness.

Anatomy of Awareness

> We may think we are aware of one, or a few, things at a time and unaware of all other things – for the time being at least…Although you are aware of innumerable things at the same time it would be wrong to imagine that you are aware of everything in the same way. Your awareness has a structure to it. (Marton and Booth 1998, 538-539)

There is a phenomenographic idea that awareness is multilayered (multi-dimensional) by nature, as seen in the above quote. That is, in being aware of something (e.g. that I am writing) it is thought that one is always simultaneously aware of other things, though not to the same degree (e.g. what, why, where I am writing) (e.g. Uljens 1996, 113). The anatomy of awareness (Marton & Booth 1997) has its roots in the work of the phenomenologist Aron Gurwitsch (1901-1973), who was a student of Edmund Husserl. The work of Gurwitsch (1964), field of consciousness, is integral to Marton's and his colleague's (ibid.) view of the anatomy (structure) of awareness, and they are seen here as parallel to each other. I prefer to start my account with the work of Gurwitsch; it sets the fundamental context of the idea, and then move on to the work of contemporary authors.

Gurwitsch (1964, 1966) developed his theory of the field of consciousness out of a background of *Gestalt* psychology and from reference to a number of other theorists, especially William James. James's notion of the stream of consciousness and its constituents laid the foundation for Gurwitsch's work. Gurwitsch (1964, 4) suggested that consciousness[4] (awareness) was made up of three overlapping areas: the margin, the thematic field and the theme[5]. The nature of experience and research into learning belong to the thematic field (Marton & Booth 1998, 539) which is therefore the main interest of this study. Gurwitsch (1966, 267-268) illustrates the total field of consciousness with a circle: "The theme …occupies the centre of this circle; it stands in the thematic field, which…forms the area of the circle; and around the thematic field…the objects of marginal consciousness are arranged." The whole idea of the field of consciousness (as well as the anatomy of awareness) is revealed by Gurwitsch (1982):

---

[4] *Gurwitsch used a term "consciousness" and therefore in quoting his texts the same concept is used here, although Marton and Booth (e.g. 1997; 1998) have used the term "awareness" for the same purpose. But other*wise *the term "awareness" is employed.*

[5] *In this study "theme", "figure" and "focus" are taken as synonymous terms as is also done with the terms "thematic field", "ground" and "background". This matches, for example, Marton and Booth's (1997) use of the same terms.*

> ...every total field of consciousness consists of three domains, each domain exhibiting a specific type of organization of its own. The first domain is the theme, that which engrosses the mind of the experiencing subject, or as it is often expressed, which stands in the 'focus of his attention.' Second is the thematic field, defined as the totality of those data, co-present with the theme, which are experienced as materially relevant or pertinent to the theme and form the background or horizon out of which the theme emerges as the center. The third includes data which, though co-present with, have no relevancy to, the theme and comprise in their totality what we propose to call the margin. (Gurwitsch 1982, 4)

Like some other phenomenographic researchers (e.g. Bruce 1992, 266; Cope 2000, 16; Arvidson 2003, 101), I, too, have designed a diagrammatic interpretation of the anatomy of awareness (Figure 3) based on the ideas of Gurwitsch (1964, 1982) and Marton and Booth (e.g. 1997), to shed more light on the core idea of a phenomenographic view of learning.

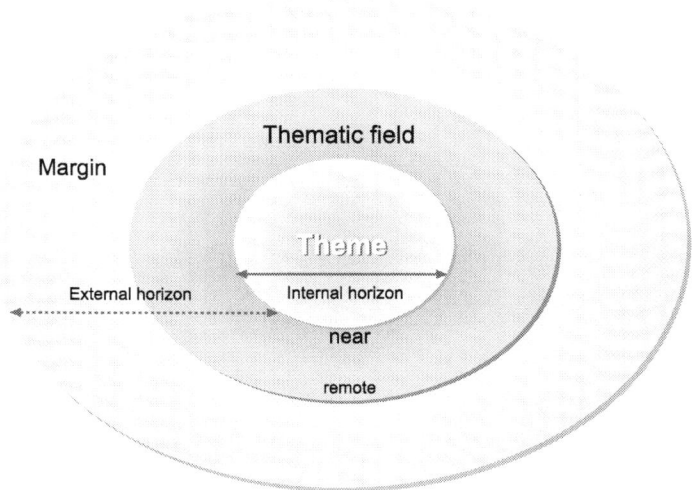

Figure 3.   A stylist view of the anatomy of awareness

From the point of view of this study the part of awareness of most interest is the theme, as it indicates what is focused on by the learner when experiencing learning. Marton (1993, 10) defines the theme of awareness in terms of the way in which it is delimited from, and related to, a context (thematic field, background) and in the way its component parts are delimited from, and related to each other, and to the whole. In other words, the theme is organised according to *Gestalt* coherence (Gurwitsch 1964, 138, 358). According to Jarvis (2004, 88) the term *Gestalt* actually means shape or form, and as early as 1912 Wertheimer claimed that the individual did not perceive the constituent elements of a phenomenon but that they are perceived as a totality.

Marton and Booth (1997, 99; see also Gurwitsch 1964, 341) suggest that the thematic field be considered in terms of constituent fields related to the theme according to relevancy. Being dynamic in nature, this relevance structure of awareness changes constantly, in accordance with an individual's changing situationality (Marton & Booth 1998, 539). In the words of Gurwitsch (1982, 3) "Every act of awareness occurs at a certain moment of time and has definite temporal relations to all other acts experienced by the same person." That is to say that our experience of a phenomenon develops through "temporally extended play between figure and ground as a function of what aspects we are focally aware of at one time" (Bowden and Marton 2004, 44). In this sense awareness has no stable content but has a stable structure (Uljens 1996, 113). Referring to that dynamic nature of awareness Arvidson (2003) uses a dance as an apt metaphor:

> ...it is not like a waltz. It is more like a variable dance with an eclectic-minded DJ – a dance at which the musical content and activities transform frequently – styles (waltz, jazz, polka, hip-hop), tempo (allegro, andante), partners (alone, group, triad), gyrations (twist, hop, lean, step), and so on. In each case of theme formation, to the extent that content is thematic or focal, it is central, consolidated, and segregated from the thematic context. (Arvidson 2003, 102)

Consequently the variation in ways of experiencing (e.g. learning) is thus a variation in ways of constituting the whole, and the parts within that whole, and the relations between those parts (Booth 2004, 12). The constituent thematic fields extend into the very life world of the learner, both backwards into his/her learning history and forwards into the way he/she continues to learn. Hence, a particular theme could have a variety of different thematic fields associated with it, depending particularly on the individual's background and intentions. Finally it is the specific thematic field generated by an individual that determines the meanings that they have for that theme. (Case 2000, 39.) As an individual's relationship with the some object continues and develops, one theme substitutes for another, being drawn from the thematic field and landing back in the thematic field (Marton & Booth 1998, 539). Gurwitsch (1964) called this a stream of consciousness. This theme-thematic field interplay is illustrated by Marton and Booth:

> Certain things come to the fore – they are figural, thematized – while other things recede to the ground – they are tacit and unthematized. And there are again, there are not two categories of awareness – figure and ground, thematized and unthematized, or explicit or implicit. There are rather different degrees of how figural, thematized, or explicit things or aspects are in your awareness. (Marton and Booth 1998, 538)

In addition to focused aspects an individual is also aware in a less focused sense of other aspects of the world, which, however, are not considered to be related to the phenomenon (e.g. Cope 2000, 16), and therefore not to belong to the theme and thematic field. That is, that there are also things that are temporally and spatially (e.g. place, time, state) coexistent in one's awareness (Marton & Booth 1998, 539). Gurwitsch (1964, 4) uses the term "margin" to refer to all that is coexistent with the theme without being related to it in the sense of same meaning.

Besides the fields of theme, thematic field and margin, a structure of awareness has also been described by Marton and Booth (1997, 87-88) in terms of an external and an internal horizon (see Figure 3 earlier). They give an illustrative metaphor concerning those horizons:

> Thus, the external horizon of coming on the deer in the woods extends from the immediate boundary of the experience – the dark forest against which the deer is distinguished – through all other contexts in which related occurrences have been experienced (e.g. walks in the forest, deer in the zoo, nursery tales, reports of hunting incidents, etc.). The internal horizon comprises the deer itself, its parts, its stance, its structural presence. (Marton & Booth 1997, 87)

In defining the horizons by means of theme, thematic field and margin, the internal horizon consists of theme and involves all the aspects of the phenomenon that are simultaneously present in the theme. In addition, that horizon implies the relationships between those aspects and the relationship between the aspects and the phenomenon as a whole. The external horizon, for one, consists of the thematic field and the margin, i.e. all aspects that are part of awareness at a particular instant but which are not thematic. The external horizon as an area of awareness forms the context in which the theme resides. That is, the border between the external and internal horizons delimits the theme from its context. (Cope 2000, 17.)

For the purposes of this study the concern is primarily with the theme (and internal horizon); what is focal in a learner's awareness in experiencing learning. According to this, a structure of awareness is delimited to the relationships between the aspects of experiencing learning that are simultaneously present in the learner's focal awareness; i.e. in the theme of his/her awareness.

Collective awareness

In addition to the interest in the individual's awareness the authors of phenomenography, particularly Bowden and Marton (e.g. 2004), have recently started to speak about collective awareness. Marton (1981) has previously called collective awareness "the collective mind". Bowden and Marton (2004) use the term "collective consciousness" but I prefer here to use the term "collective awareness" because it is congruent with Marton and Booth's (1997) anatomy of awareness and also with my use of that term throughout the book. Furthermore, according to my understanding, consciousness, in the sense in which the term is used in this research, is rather individual than collective. Consequently here the term "aware" is used instead of the term "conscious".

Bowden and Marton's (2004) framework of the university as a learning community involves both learning at an individual level and learning at a collective level. From the phenomenographic point of view learning at a collective level can be understood in terms of collective awareness, i.e. individuals' awarenesses are linked to each other, forming collective awareness (ibid., 190).

According to Bowden and Marton (ibid., 206) collective awareness emerges when different people are aware of the same phenomenon and are aware as well to a greater or lesser extent, of each others' ways of experiencing, seeing, thinking about that phenomenon. Bowden and Marton (ibid., 189) suggest that if we become aware of others' ways of experiencing something, then we have a certain degree of collective awareness.

From the point of view of learning, collective awareness has some advantages in addition to individual awareness. Collective awareness implies (Bowden & Marton ibid., 201) that when we become aware of someone else's experiencing of a certain phenomenon our own experiencing of the phenomenon is likely to be enriched. And, further, when we become aware of someone else's experiencing of a certain phenomenon this experiencing relates to our knowledge about the world (which surely is more or less different from what the other person knows about the world), therefore the very insight we become aware of is enriched. Thus, enrichment is reciprocal.

Collective awareness feeds on individual capabilities, but the converse is also true. The richer and the more interconnected the collective awareness is, the more likely it is that the variation both between and within individual capability will increase (the way of experiencing a certain phenomenon becomes more complex and complete). (Bowden & Marton 2004, 204.) By linking different ways of experiencing we gain a fuller understanding of the world and the phenomenon to be learned. In keeping with this, Bowden and Marton (2004, 209) suggest that studying (learning) should strive to increase collective awareness by means of pooling individuals' ideas, thoughts and ways of experiencing phenomena of shared interest. Associated with collective awareness one should note here, as mentioned in Chapter 1, that phenomenography does not describe the variation in individual experience but the variation in the experience of individuals as a collective (e.g. Prosser 2005, 7).

Experience

Since, experience plays a markedly dominant role in a phenomenographic view of learning, and consequently in this study, the characteristics of that issue are discussed below in greater detail.

In his very experiencing the human being adopts a relationship to the world. (Rauhala 1981, 90). In keeping with this idea, experience refers to the internal relationship between the person experiencing and the phenomenon experienced (Marton & Booth 1997, 108). This internal relationship exists because awareness is structured, as discussed previously in this chapter, in such a way that certain things come to the fore whereas others recede to the background (Marton 1992, 9). According to Jarvis (2004, 94) experience is a continuous lifelong phenomenon rather than an episode, although there are also episodic incidents that relate to our awareness. Therefore, experience usually refers to immediate experience or experiencing; the kind of experience that every moment of life is full of, i.e. immediate, engaged beingness or life as lived through (Uljens 1997, 29). Experience always presents us with objects, things, events, etc., within certain contexts (situations), and never with isolated and scattered data and facts (Gurwitsch 1982, 1). On the one hand experience belongs to an individual but on other hand it also implies a collective dimension, as became apparent in the previous section. Olesen (1996) brings in the collective part of experience (the word in parentheses is mine):

> Experience is the process whereby we as human beings, individually and collectively, consciously master reality, and the ever-living understanding of this reality and our relation to it....Experience is thus a subjective process as it is seen from the point of view of the person experiencing. It is also a collective process because when we experience as individuals, we also do so through a socially structured consciousness [awareness]. (Olesen 1996, 8)

The experiences are inexhaustible and based on people's earlier experience. Husserl (1973) illustrates this in his statement below:

> Depending on my particular goals, I may have enough of what an experience has already provided me, and the "I just break off" with an "It is enough." However; I can convince myself that no determination is the last that which has already been experienced always still has, without limit, a horizon of possible experience of the same. (Husserl 1973, 32 cited in Moustakas 1994, 55)

According to Dewey (1963 cited in Illeris 2002, 148) experience has two dimensions which are particularly salient for education. Those dimensions are continuity and interaction. The dimension of continuity of experience means that every experience both takes up something from those that have gone before and modifies in some way the quality of those that come after (Dewey 1963, 35). The dimension of transaction takes place between an individual and what, at the same time, constitutes his/her situationality (ibid., 43).

The same dimensions of experience are delimited slightly differently by Clandinin and Connelly (1994, 417) focusing experience in four dimensions: inward and outward, backward and forward. Inward refers to the internal conditions of feelings, hopes, aesthetic reactions, moral dispositions, and so on. Outward refers to existential conditions, i.e. the environment (reality). By backward and forward refer to time, past, present and future. Due to temporality, it is only in relation to our previous experience that a new experience can be unexpected and it is only in relation to a new experience that our previous experience is defined as existing (Uljens 1997, 30-31). To experience an experience is to experience it simultaneously in these four ways. In the phenomenographic view of learning all these four dimensions are taken into account.

Experience plays an essential role in a human being's sense-making. Experience is "the totality of ways in which human beings either make, or try to make, sense of what they consciously perceive" (Jarvis 2004, 104). Therefore, as noted by Rauhala (1981, 109), wherever in the human sciences the object is to study experiencing and in application to influence it, the problem encountered is the problem of meaning. The basic premise is that human beings create meanings out of their experiences and act, or try to act, in accordance with those meanings (Pohland & Bova 2000, 138). Giorgi (2005, 82) elaborates the relationship between meaning and experience by stating that "…the meaning is not a third term between the act and object, but the particular way that object is experienced." This process of sense-making is precisely what is entailed for the world's phenomena and their interrelationships to mean something to us. Phenomena exist for us experientially in as much as the senses appear to us from them. Due to this, the world is primarily given to us meaningfully in experiencing. (Rauhala 1981, 89.)

To sum up, using a concept of "a way of experiencing something" in phenomenography and describing how something is experienced, is a description of the meaning that this something has for the human being. Depending on different situations, this something may also have different meanings for the same human being. What meaning it has for a human being could be understood in terms of which aspects of the object are discerned and held in focal awareness simultaneously. (Runesson & Mok 2004, 63.) The matter of discerning and simultaneity are included in a phenomenographic theory of variation, which will be discussed later in Section 4.1.2.

Intentionality

Despite the fact that phenomenographers do not concur with mental models of learning, it is, however, fundamental to an understanding of the phenomenographic view of learning to recognise that its epistemological stance is premised on the principle of intentionality of awareness (e.g. Uljens 1996; Marton & Booth 1997). Husserl's concept of intentionality, which he in turn attributed to Franz Brentano (1838-1917) (Niiniluoto & Saarinen 2002, 218), is evident in the very essence of phenomenography and its goals and approaches to exploring phenomena as experienced by people (see e.g. Marton & Booth 1997, 84-86). By intentionality Husserl meant that every act of awareness takes an object that transcends the act (Giorgi 2005, 76).

Intentionality in a broad sense has been taken to mean that human beings' awareness is always directed towards something other than itself (e.g. Uljens 1996, 106), i.e. it has an object. Dennet (1997, 42) explains that something demonstrates intentionality if its ability is, one way or another, related to something else. Thus, intentionality denotes that awareness must be understood in terms of what a subject is aware of in being aware of something (ibid.).

According to Niiniluoto (1983, 368) the word intentionality is derived from the Latin term "intendere", which means orientation. In its philosophical meaning, intentionality is simply being a part of something (aboutness) (Dennet 1997, 43). The philosophers of the Middle Ages developed the term while noticing that this phenomenon is similar to the aiming of the arrow of a bow. That is to say, that an intentional phenomenon is, in a way, equipped with a symbolic arrow which is aimed at something, whatever the phenomenon aims at. The target of thinking, whether real or not, was called by those theorists the object of intentionality. (ibid.)

In a famous passage Brentano (1995) claimed that every mental state and event has intentionality:

> Every mental phenomenon is characterized by what the Scholastics of the Middle Ages called the intentional (or mental) inexistence of an object, and what we might call, though not wholly unambiguously, reference to a content, direction toward an object (which is not to be understood here as

> meaning a thing), or immanent objectivity. In presentation something is presented, in judgment something is affirmed or denied, in love loved, in hate hated, in desire desired, and so on. (Brentano 1995, 88)

Rauhala (1989, 128) has summed up Husserl's concepts of intention and intentionality regarding learning:

- intention is a characteristic referring to the external object of the contents of the act of awareness
- the function of intentionality is to implement the fulfilment of meaning, or to assemble the contents given in act observation
- intention refers to the birth of meaning, with which the external object is summarised (and at the same time intended)
- intention has the function of intersubjective meaning giving and meaning creation (meanings that are distinguished from psychic activities)
- intention constitutes the being as an aware consciousness and is thus involved in the birth of the world view.

Ruohotie (2005a, 6) characterises that intentional learners are not only cognitively committed to the learning process, but they also monitor and adjust their learning and their actions are guided by motives, goals, beliefs and emotions.

From the perspective of phenomenography the notion of intentionality is treated in terms of the "what" and "how" dimensions of the phenomenon. The previous idea denotes that when a human being is aware, he/she is always aware of something (what) and he or she is aware of this something in some way (how). (Uljens 1996, 108; Marton & Booth 1997, 84.) Thus a phenomenon, for example learning, has two objects, the direct object (the what dimension) and the indirect object (the how dimension) (Marton & Booth 1997, 84).

4.1.2 Theory of Variation

> There is no learning without discernment. And there is no discernment without variation. (Marton & Trigwell 2000, 381)

As suggested, for example by Booth & Hulten (2003, 69), the phenomenographic tradition has grown a theoretical framework for approaching learning. This framework is entitled a theory of variation (Marton & Booth 1997; Bowden & Marton 2004; Marton & Tsui 2004). The theory makes use of the anatomy of awareness, discussed previously in Section 4.1.1.

In keeping with its name, the theory puts strong emphasise on variation as epistemologically fundamental to all learning. It is claimed by Marton and Trigwell (2000, 394; see also Bowden & Marton 2004; Marton & Tsui 2004) that when it comes to preparing learners for an unknown future, the nature of variation is of crucial importance. Marton, Runesson and Tsui (2004, 15) namely believe that variation enables learners to experience the features that are critical for a particular learning as well as for the development of certain capabilities.

The theory of variation assumes as its basic principle that for learning to occur, variation must be experienced by the learner (e.g. Marton & Trigwell 2000, 381). The cornerstones of the theory are the concepts "discernment", "variation", and "simultaneity" (e.g. Marton & Tsui 2004). Consequently, in order to learn the learner must experience the world in terms of discernment, variation and simultaneity (e.g. Bowden & Marton 2004, 8).

According to the theory the most important kind of education is the one that attempts to develop in the learner powerful ways of experiencing the world (e.g. Bowden & Marton 2004; Marton & Tsui 2004). This implies that in order to experience the world in a powerful way, the learner must be able to discern certain critical aspects of the world (i.e. aspects that are relevant and necessary for handling a situation effectively). These aspects have to be in relation to the context (situation) at hand, and in addition to this the learner must become aware of the aspects simultaneously. However, to reach this stage the learner ought to experience variation in aspects of the phenomenon. In other words, variation is a prerequisite for all kinds of discernment to happen. (Marton, Runesson & Tsui 2004, 10-20.) As exemplified by Marton and Trigwell (2000, 386), darkness can only be discerned and experienced as a contrast to light. Or, in the same line of reasoning, one cannot discern greenness without the experience of other colours, i.e. without variation in colours the very idea of colour does not exist at all.

With regard to the above line of reasoning it can be thought that a lack in experiencing the world in a powerful way is then linked to being unaware of variation in the world, or the learner is experiencing just that which he/she takes for granted (Booth & Hulten 2003, 70). It is assumed by Jarvis (2004, 92) that taken-for-grantedness lies in the fact that people are in harmony with their socio-cultural environment. Based on that, people do not have to think deeply before they act, because they seem instinctively to know how to act in particular circumstances. This is not, however, intuitive but the result of previous learning experiences, states Jarvis (ibid.). Hence, the difference in the kind of variations invoked in a learning situation will result in qualitatively different kinds of learning experiences (Ki & Lam et al. 2003, 56).

According to Marton and Trigwell (2000, 386) discerning something, however, is not the same as constructing something that is not there in the world. Nor is it picking up something which is there independently without the human being's act of discernment. On the contrary, it means that an aspect of the world appears to the learner, and is experienced by him/her against the background of his/her previous experiences of something more or less different. In Booth and Hulten's (2003, 69) words discernment is "the act of seeing this no-longer-taken-for-granted phenomenon or aspect of a phenomenon in a new light."

Marton et al. (2004, 16-17, see also Turunen 1998, 85) identify four patterns of variation needed for effective discernment. Firstly, in order to experience something, one must experience something else to contrast it with. For example, to be aware of what "three" is a person must experience something that is not three; "two" or "four", for instance. Secondly, following the previous example, in order to fully understand what "three" is, one must also experience varying the appearances of "three", for instance three people, three adults, etc. This is called generalization. Thirdly, to experience a certain aspect and to separate this aspect from other aspects, the certain aspect must vary while others remain constant. And fourthly, in the case of numerous critical aspects that the learner has to consider at the same time, they must all be experienced simultaneously.

Simultaneity, as one of the cornerstones of the theory, is taken by Marton et al. (2004, 17-19) to mean that, in order to experience variation in a certain respect, one has to experience the different aspects that vary in that respect simultaneously. In other words, one has to experience those aspects that he/she has encountered at different points in time, at the same time. Such simultaneity is known as diachronic simultaneity. Marton et al. (ibid.) call the other type of simultaneity synchronic simultaneity, denoting the experience of different co-existing aspects of the same thing at the same time.

Summing up the theory of variation, the limited number of qualitatively different ways of experiencing something are, according to the theory, to be understood with regard to the discernment of aspects, the simultaneity of aspects discerned and the potential for variation in discerned aspects of the phenomenon in question (Marton & Fai 1999). Hence, it is possible in phenomenography to describe a way of experiencing a phenomenon in terms of the critical aspects of the phenomenon in question (here learning) discerned and focused on simultaneously by the experiencer (here learner). Bringing the theory of variation into practice of formal learning Runesson and Mok (2004; see also Runesson 1999) suggest that excellence in teaching has very much to do with what aspects of what is meant to be learned are subjected to variation, and even more, what aspects of the phenomenon are subject to variation simultaneously.

4.2 Comparison of Learning Perspectives

To find out how the phenomenographic perspective on learning is situated in the field of other prevailing learning perspectives, some comparisons are needed. While it is not the aim of this study to cover all learning theories recently used in education, the comparison is restricted to constructivism.

According to Tynjälä (1999a, 363), constructivism is a theory of knowing. There are, however, varieties of constructivism (see for instance Phillips, 1995). As is also recognised by Tynjälä (ibid., 363-364), "constructivism is not a unified theory, but rather a conglomeration of different positions with varying emphases". The original core of constructivism locates it in psychological theory about how beliefs are developed but has expanded to include philosophical, educational as well as sociological constructivism (Matthews 1997, 6-7). Similarly, referring to the literature on constructivism, Tynjälä (1999a, 364) has found it includes at least the following branches: radical or cognitive constructivism, social constructivism, the sociocultural approach, symbolic interactionism, and social constructionism. She deems that the common denominator to these various strands is that the acquisition of knowledge is metaphorically described as a building process in which knowledge is actively constructed whether by individuals or social communities. Accordingly, the difference between them lies in the role they assign to the individual and the social part in learning. (ibid.)

The kind of constructivism this study is interested in here is that of educational constructivism, which, according to Matthews (1997, 7), divides it into personal (also called individual constructivism or cognitive constructivism or radical constructivism) and social constructivism, which are the two broad strands of constructivism. Whereas cognitive or radical constructivist (individual) thinking places emphasise on individuals' knowledge construction processes and mental models, social constructivists or constructionists are more interested in social, dialogical, and collaborative processes (Tynjälä 1999a, 364; see also Matthews 1997; Puolimatka 2002a).

The stream of individual constructivism has its origins in Piaget's (1983) genetic epistemology and von Glasersfeld (1995), proposing radical constructivism, is perhaps its most famous representative (Matthews 1997, 7). Individual constructivism claims that knowledge is not passively acquired from the outside world or implanted as an a priori representation in the mind, but is constructed by the mind's ability to actively explore and develop its own meaningful accounts of phenomena. The source of knowledge is generated from individuals' previous and concurrent interactions with their social and physical environments and through their ability to reason about and symbolically transform these interactions into personally constructed interpretations. Knowledge of a phenomenon is subsequently represented as a conceptual or symbolic interpretation that conveys meaning for the individual. Differences in meaning are characterised as different interpretations of the same phenomenon and are related to variations in individuals' conceptual abilities. Changes in meaning are understood as the ability to develop more complex interpretations that match individuals' changing needs. (Watkins 2000, 97-98, see also Tynjälä 1999b; Puolimatka 2002a.)

Social constructivists, for their part, emphasise the making of knowledge by society of individuals rather than by individuals. Consequently, knowledge is seen as a collaborative intersubjective construction and is appropriated by individuals from the socially organised practices of the group in which they participate. Thus, knowledge or meaning is embedded in participatory forms of social practice and is subject to the structuring influences of historical processes and sociocultural beliefs that surround these practices. Differences in meaning are subsequently held to represent variations in social practice and reflect different normative beliefs held by different groups. Changes in meaning are associated with evolving social practices and indicate individuals' increasing enculturation in these practices. (Watkins 2000, 99.) Constructivism of the social variety has its origins in Vygotsky's (1978) work in linguistics and language acquisition (Matthews 1997, 7; see also Tynjälä 1999b; Puolimatka 2002a.)

Marton and Booth (1997, 6-13) categorically reject both individual and social constructivism. Similarly, Prosser and Trigwell (1999, 13) state that a non-dualistic perspective, advocated in phenomenography, is fundamentally different from other, such as individual and social constructivist, perspectives of learning. Thus, phenomenography has refrained from positing any cognitivistic explanations or mental models of cognition. Instead it argues that human understanding is inevitably a human-world relation. (Pong 1999.) By defining humans and the world as inextricably intertwined phenomenography transcends the person-world dichotomy suggested by the traditions of both individual and social constructivism (Marton & Booth 1997, 83).

The phenomenographic research on learning is based within a constitutionalist framework that differs from a constructivist framework on humans' activity. The constitutive framework in phenomenography goes beyond internalism (individual constructivism) and externalism (social constructivism). Experience is seen as internal relationships between the individuals and their surroundings, described in terms of learners' meanings of objects. (Anderberg 2000, 7.) Tynjälä (1999a, 364) takes the view that although cognitive or radical (individual) constructivism is distinct from the phenomenographic view of learning, there are fundamental resemblances between social constructivist views and those of phenomenographic. Finally, Biggs (2003, 15) postulates that both constructivism and phenomenography emphasise learners as knowledge creators. No matter if it is called constructing knowledge or constituting knowledge. Biggs claims that the point is that knowledge is not imposed or transmitted by direct instruction.

Lave (1996) has proposed that at minimum a theory of learning consists of three kinds of stipulations which are Telos, subject-world relation and learning mechanisms:

- Telos: a direction of movement or change of learning
- subject-world relation: a general specification of relations between subjects and the social world
- learning mechanisms: ways by which learning comes about. (ibid.)

To recapitulate and to compare the core features of phenomenographic, individual constructivist and social constructivist perspectives on learning and to summarise the section, the different perspectives are captured applying Lave's (ibid.) stipulations in Table 1.

Table 1. *Comparison of phenomenography, individual constructivism and social constructivism*

	Phenomenography	Individual constructivism	Social constructivism
Telos	Change in the structure of individual's awareness	Change in individuals mental models	Changes in meaning associated with social practices
Subject-world relation	Non-dualistic; there is one world, that of experienced	Dualistic; there is an independent reality	Dualistic/non-dualistic
Mechanism	Constitution of knowledge through variation, discernment, simultaneity	Knowledge is actively constructed by individuals, not passively received	Construction of knowledge through language and discourse and participation in social practices

5 METHODOLOGICAL UNDERPINNINGS

This chapter locates the study in a qualitative research paradigm, outlines the major assumptions associated with the phenomenographic research approach and compares this approach with certain other methods. In so doing the chapter aims to provide justification for the choice of the research approach applied. In this study in connection with phenomenography I use the term approach or research approach, instead of the frequently used terms method, methodology, paradigm and framework.

5.1 Determining the Research Approach

A research method offers a systematic way of accomplishing the study in an orderly and a disciplined manner. The different procedures or techniques which make up a method provide both the direction and the steps to be followed. In so doing they also move the study into action. (Moustakas 1994, 104.) The determining of suitable method(s) is based on the ontological, epistemological as well as theoretical assumptions of the object and the purpose of the study (see Chapters 1, 3, 4 and Figure 1). This is to say that the decision depends on the nature of the phenomenon studied and the knowledge interest the researcher is pursuing. An elaboration of these premises leads the researcher in a particular methodological direction.

As presented in Chapter 1, the ultimate aim of this study is to contribute to basic research concerning the learning of adults studying alongside their work in a university setting and methods of exploring that learning. It should be noted here that the research addresses the learners' perceptions of their learning experiences and therefore does not even try to distinguish actual (real) learning from perceived learning. In other words, the phenomenon this research is interested in is adult learners' learning (the subject of the research), for which knowledge and understanding are sought through learners' ways of experiencing (unit and object of the research) their learning.

The research addresses the following three research questions:

1. What kind of variation is there in adult learners' ways of experiencing their learning at a university?
2. What kind of a holistic view (an outcome space) can be constituted from adult learners' various ways of experiencing their learning at a university?
3. What kind of research approach is phenomenography in investigating adult learners' experiences of their learning at a university?

5.1.1 Criteria for the Choice of Approach

As mentioned at the beginning of the chapter, a qualitative research methodology was employed in this study. The main reason for a qualitative approach is condensed in Husén's (1997, 17) argumentation that a paradigm that seeks causal explanations derives from the natural sciences and emphasises "empirical quantifiable observations", whereas a paradigm that focuses on understanding, as is the case here, "is derived from the humanities with emphasis on holistic and qualitative information and interpretive approaches". My choice of a qualitative paradigm is also supported by Giorgi (2005, 80). He argues that when asking a question that relates to what it is like to experience a particular phenomenon, one should use a qualitative method. Giorgi claims that an experience does not have any quantitative structure that will defend quantitative methods. According to him such logic is immaculate. In addition to the arguments presented above, my personal preferences also inclined towards a qualitative approach.

Giorgi (2005, 80) points out that a good research design follows the sense of investigation and should therefore not in an a priori way determine what methods are to be used. Instead, it is crucial to consciously select an approach, since "different approaches offer varying perspectives on the research questions and serve to lead the researcher on different roads" (Berglund 2005, 35). Taking the above recommendations as well as my object, purpose and research questions into account, I set the following requirements, which the research approach should at least meet. It should

- allow adult learners' individual and collective voices to be heard
- allow access to adult learners' lived experience concerning their learning
- allow variations in adult learners' lived experience to come to light
- allow description of the adult learners' experiences of learning
- allow a holistic view of the phenomena of experiencing learning
- contribute to the research and practice of adults' learning.

Therefore, before deciding which qualitative method would be the most appropriate for the present study, several approaches were contemplated. There were three different methodological approaches in particular which were at a first glance thought to be suitable for the study. The approaches included phenomenology (e.g. Moustakas 1994; Giorgi 1999, 2005), phenomenography (e.g. Marton 1978, 1981, 1994a, 1997; Marton & Booth 1997), and grounded theory (e.g. Glaser & Strauss 1967; Strauss & Corbin 1994; Charmaz 2000). They are all qualitative research designs that guide human science research and are claimed to provide access to individual experience. As has become apparent throughout the preceding chapters, phenomenography was eventually the selected approach. The reasons for rejecting other approaches are presented. This argumentation calls for a comparison of the three methods. Table 2 (in Chapter 5.1.2) brings the methods side by side to reveal their distinct features from the point of interest of the present study. However, first the salient features of phenomenology and grounded theory are briefly discussed below. The detailed description of the chosen approach, phenomenography, is finally to be found in Section 5.2.

5.1.2 Comparison of Alternative Methods

Phenomenology

There are many articles dealing with the relationships between phenomenology and phenomenography (see e.g. Giorgi 1986, 1999; Hasselgren & Beach 1997; Uljens 1996; Richardson 1999; Marton & Booth 1997; Ashworth & Lucas 2000; Niikko 2003; Latomaa 2005). In all of them the authors have come to the conclusion that despite many shared values, differences in understanding and in practice between of the two approaches exist (see e.g. Giorgi 1999). In the following I will briefly elucidate both of them.

Phenomenology came into being as a philosophy initiated by Edmund Husserl. According to Giorgi (1999) this implies that when doing phenomenological research the researcher must first position herself within the framework of phenomenological philosophy. The aim of the empirical phenomenological approach is defined by Moustakas (1994, 13) as involving "a return to experience in order to obtain a comprehensive description that provides the basis for a reflective structural analysis that portrays the essence of the experience." Van Manen (1990, 19) completes the idea by proposing that "[p]henomenology appeals to our immediate common experience in order to conduct a structural analysis of what is most common, most familiar, most self evident to us."

As conceded by Marton and Booth (1997, 117), phenomenography has some relationship to phenomenology, but according to them it is, at best, like a-cousin-by-marriage relationship. Giorgi (1999), on the contrary, claims that in terms of its origins and inspiration phenomenography is closer to phenomenology than Marton and Booth (ibid.) acknowledge. Both approaches use parallel concepts, such as phenomenon, experience, awareness, intentionality, bracketing, external and internal horizons, noema, noesis and so on. However, in most cases the concepts are used differently within each approach.

With regard to learning the shared values of phenomenography and phenomenology are presented by Giorgi (1999), as follows

- both value a strictly qualitative approach to the problem of learning
- both insist that comprehending the perspective of the learner is crucial
- both acknowledge that there are various ways in which human beings can perceive or understand a phenomenon and situation
- both approaches claim to be descriptive in orientation
- both claim some influence of phenomenological philosophy; phenomenography claims a distant influence whereas the phenomenological psychological approach claims to be fully and explicitly influenced (ibid.).

Although phenomenography and phenomenology have much in common, they differ as to their purpose (Marton 1996b) and in the ways they go about the enterprise (Marton and Booth 1997, 116). Whereas phenomenography, with its suffix "graph" wants to describe that which comes to light, phenomenology, with its suffix "logos", wants to draw together that which is manifest in order to clarify its logic or structure (Giorgi 1999). Therefore, in phenomenology, the search for a singular essence or the most invariant of a phenomenon becomes central, while in phenomenography the main point is, on the contrary, to find the variation of the world as experienced (Marton 1996b). Hence, especially, the focus of phenomenographic research, the variation in other peoples' experiences of the phenomena and the architecture of the variation, contrasts with phenomenology, which tries to develop a single theory of experience (Marton & Booth 1997, 116-117).

Finally, phenomenology was not deemed suitable for the study particularly because it concentrates on the singular essence (invariance) of experience of phenomenon, but not on the variation in experiencing the phenomenon. Additionally, it also places emphasis on individuals' experience, but not on that of the collective. And therefore it did not provide the required holistic view of the phenomena of experiencing learning within the sample group.

Grounded theory

Grounded theory is defined by Charmaz (2004, 6396) as "an inductive methodology that provides systematic guidelines for gathering, synthesizing, analyzing, and conceptualizing qualitative data for the purpose of theory construction." In the same spirit Strauss and Corbin (1994, 273) describe grounded theory as "a general methodology for developing theory that is grounded in data systematically gathered and analysed." Thus, as can easily be seen, the term "grounded theory" stems from its fundamental principle; theory has to be developed via systematic analysis of empirical data (Charmaz 2004, 6396).

Grounded theory was presented initially by Glaser and Strauss (1967). Its roots are in symbolic interactionism (Blumer 1969), which itself derives from the pragmatist ideas of James, Dewey and Mead (Heath & Cowley 2004, 142). Interactionism states that individuals are self-aware, able to see themselves from the perspective of others and therefore to adapt their behaviour according to the situation (Heath & Cowley 2004, 142 referring to Mead 1934).

Richardson (1999, 70-71) points out that several authors (Entwistle & Ramsden 1983; Säljö 1988; Francis 1993) have noted the similarity between phenomenography and grounded theory. Richardson (ibid., 68.) himself, as well as other authors, link the techniques of data analysis employed in phenomenographic research to those of grounded theory. Those techniques are claimed by Charmaz (2004, 6396; 2005, 508) to imply: simultaneous data collection and analysis, making of constant comparisons, early development of categories, intermediate analytic writing between coding data and writing the first draft, sampling for developing ideas, delay of the literature review, and a thrust toward developing theory. While grounded theory uses slightly similar techniques as phenomenography, it differs, for instance, with regard to interviews in two aspects. Firstly, in grounded theory only excerpts from transcripts are analysed, rather than whole transcripts. Secondly, grounded theory is often approached from a perspective which probes the unconscious intent of an interviewee (Dunkin 2000 referring to Cherry 1998), rather than an integrated situational and personal (relational) focus that is the hallmark of phenomenography (see Marton & Booth 1997). In addition, Trigwell (2000) sees the

Table 2. *Comparison of a phenomenographic approach, phenomenology and grounded theory*

Object of comparison	Phenomenographic research approach	Phenomenology	Grounded theory
What is it?	An empirical study of the limited number of qualitatively different ways in which we experience, conceptualise, understand, etc., various phenomena in and aspects of the world around us (Marton & Booth 1997, 95)	A program of developing a single theory of experience by using a particular method, which, befitting the philosophy, is a philosophical method. (Marton & Booth 1997, 116)	A general methodology for developing theory that is grounded in data systematically gathered and analysed (Strauss & Corbin 1994, 273)
Aim	To reveal the qualitatively different ways of experiencing various phenomena (Marton & Booth 1997, 136)	To reveal more fully the essence and meanings of human experiences (Moustakas 1994, 105)	To develop at various levels of theory, mostly a substantive theory (Strauss & Corbin 1994, 273)
Research question	What are the qualitatively different ways of experiencing a phenomenon? (Marton & Booth 1997, 136)	How do people perceive and describe their experience of something (e.g. learning)? (Moustakas 1994, 106)	What is something (e.g. learning) in this situation and under specific conditions? (Strauss & Corbin 1994, 276)
Focus on	Variations in ways people experience the phenomenon (Marton & Booth 1997, 121)	The essence of experience (Moustakas 1994, 13)	Theory development (Strauss & Corbin 1994, 274)
Source of data	Typically an interview at a state of meta-awareness (Marton & Booth 132)	Typically a long interview (Moustakas 1994, 114)	Interview, field observations, documents of all types, videotapes (Strauss & Corbin 1994, 274)
Analytic tools	The analysis is strongly iterative and comparative in nature (Åkerlind 2005b, 321) and takes advantage of the anatomy of awareness (Marton & Booth 1997)	The processes of Epoché and phenomenological reduction (Moustakas 1994, 60)	Data-theory interplay, making of constant comparisons, asking of theoretically oriented questions, theoretical coding (Strauss & Corbin 1994, 283)
Theory generation	Post data collection (Hales & Watkins 2004)	During and post data collection (Hales & Watkins 2004)	During the research process and from the data being collected (Moustakas 1994, 4)
Research outcomes	Categories of description and an outcome space denoting the logical relationship between the categories, i.e. collective anatomy of awareness (Marton & Booth 1997, 136)	A unified statement of the essence of the experience of the phenomena as a whole. The essences of any experience are never totally exhausted (Moustakas 1994, 100)	Grounded theories; substantive theory (grounded in research on one particular substantive area) and formal theory (Strauss & Corbin 1994, 281)
Validity	How well the research outcomes correspond to human experience of the phenomenon (Uljens 1996)	When the knowledge sought is arrived at through descriptions that make possible an understanding of the meaning and essences of experiences (Moustakas 1994, 84)	As conditions change, this affects the validity of theories – that is, their relation to contemporary reality (Strauss & Corbin 1994, 274)
Generalization	To the extent the sample group represents the variation of individuals in a wider population (or is a theoretical sample of that population) the categories of description can also be said to apply to the wider population (Marton & Booth 1997, 124)	Limited to the time, situation and the researcher (Hales and Watkins 2004)	If approximately similar conditions exist, approximately similar consequences should occur (Strauss & Corbin 1994, 278)

Finally, a phenomenographic approach was construed as particularly well suited to the purpose of the research, namely, to identify variability in learners ways of experiencing learning (research question one), and to constitute a holistic view of the phenomenon of experiencing learning (research question two).

The key features of a phenomenographic research approach are described below. However, one should take into account that this description is made from the methodological perspective while Chapter 4 discusses phenomenography from the perspective of learning.

5.2 The Phenomenographic Research Approach

Supposedly the most often quoted definition for the phenomenographic research approach is that of Marton's (e.g. 1997, 95), which presents phenomenography as an "empirical study of the limited number of qualitatively different ways in which various phenomena in, and aspects of, the world around us are experienced, conceptualized, understood, perceived, and apprehended." In focusing on qualitatively different ways of experiencing phenomena the definition suits the aim of the present study. The definition clearly reveals the basic principle behind all phenomenographic investigations. The principle indicates "that whatever phenomenon or situation people encounter, it is possible to identify a limited number of qualitatively different and logically interrelated ways in which the phenomenon or the situation is experienced" (Marton 1997, 97).

The methodological underpinnings of the phenomenographic research approach were articulated by Marton in the late 1970s (Marton 1978) and early 1980s (Marton 1981; Marton 1986). Although, as an evolving research approach phenomenography has in the course of time undergone many renewals and refinements, its basic idea has remained stable. Therefore, it is necessary to some extent to review its roots and origins. In the early days Marton (1978, 6) wrote that "[t]he kind of research we wish to argue ...is research which aims at description, analysis, and understanding of experiences; that is, research which is directed towards experiential description." He elaborated the kind of research further as a programme, the aim of which is "not to classify people, nor is it to compare groups, to explain, to predict, nor to make fair or unfair judgements of people. It is to find and systematize forms of thought in terms of which people interpret aspects of reality" (ibid). The description above likely resembles qualitative research at a general level and as opposed to quantitative research. In these early works Marton did not yet use the term "phenomenography".

About twenty years ago the term phenomenography was already in use and Marton (1986, 31) defined the approach as "a research method adapted for mapping the qualitative different ways in which people experience, conceptualise, perceive, and understand various aspects of, and phenomena in, the world around them." This definition has very much in common with today's phenomenographic approach. The emphasis is on how things appear to people in their world and the way in which people explain to themselves and others what goes on around them and how these explanations change (Barnard, McCosker & Gerber 1999, 214).

Finally, Marton and Booth (1997) redefined phenomenography in their book *Learning and Awareness*, which contains the most precise description of the idea of phenomenography:

> Phenomenography is not a method in itself, although there are methodological elements associated with it…Phenomenography is rather a way of - an approach to – identifying, formulating, and tackling certain sort of research questions, a specialization that is particularly aimed at questions of relevance to learning and understanding in an educational setting. (Marton and Booth 1997, 111)

By methodological elements Marton and Booth (ibid.) refer to empirical data collection and the analysis of that data. When comparing the last two definitions, a phenomenographic movement towards a more holistic theoretical framework, particularly in relation to an educational setting, becomes apparent. In the past phenomenography was more just a pattern for analysing qualitative data, but today (as described in Chapter 4) it is also a theory of learning.

From the point of view of Marton (e.g. 1996) and his fellow researchers (e.g. Marton & Booth 1997) phenomenography is therefore not a method, but rather a set of assumptions about humans, about science and about how we can acquire knowledge about other peoples' ways of experiencing the world (Sjöström & Dahlgren 2002, 339). It argues for a relational non-dualistic view of learning (discussed in more detail in Chapter 3), and is influenced by the *Gestalt* psychologists' view on whole qualities (Wertheimer, 1945; Gurwitsch, 1964) (discussed in more detail in Section 4.1.1).

Lately, phenomenographers have started to speak about two kinds of phenomenographic approaches; the traditional and the new one. Whereas the traditional approach aims to investigate the qualitatively different ways in which people experience the world around them (Marton & Pong 2005, 335), the new phenomenography also focuses on people's awareness of patterns of variation and ways of bringing about variation (McKenzie 2003, 79). In other words, the new approach makes use of the anatomy of awareness (see Section 4.1.1) and thereby focuses on describing ways of experiencing in terms of the experiencing individual's awareness of critical aspects and related dimensions in variation (ibid). Despite the phenomenographic development, both the traditional and the new approach share a common focus on variation and experience with the basic assumption that a way of experiencing a phenomenon is a relation between the individual and reality. (see e.g. Marton 1981; Marton & Booth 1997.) There are studies which combine the traditional phenomenographic approach with additional, new phenomenographical focus on analysing the dimensions of variation as experienced (see e.g. Pong 1999). This combined phenomenographic mode matches well with, and is used in, the present study.

5.2.1 The Object of the Phenomenographic Approach

In attempting to delineate an object of his/her research, a phenomenographic researcher is faced with some confusion regarding the terminology used in relation to the object of the research. For that purpose there are many synonymously used terms, the most frequent being "concept" and "conception" or "experience" and "ways of experiencing". Marton and Booth (1997, 111), for example, state that, "the unit of phenomenographic research is a way of experiencing something...and the object of the research is the variation in ways of experiencing phenomena." But, in their recent paper Marton and Pong (2005, 335-336) label a concept, "also called as ways of conceptualizing, experiencing, seeing, apprehending, understanding and so on," as the basic unit of description in phenomenography. They argue for their use of interchangeable terms by stating that although none of them match totally with what they have in mind, they all do so to certain extend. It is, however, admitted by Marton and Pong that the term "conceptualizing" is not identical with the term "experiencing". According to them the idea of separating the terms is that one can discern and focus upon the conceptual features of a phenomenon just as one can discern and focus on the sense-related features of a phenomenon. In addition, Marton (1996a, 172-173) takes the view that the term "way of experiencing" is more generic in nature than either the above-listed synonyms, at least when it comes to phenomenographic phraseology. In conclusion, Marton (1996a, 173) recommends that the researcher should use the more appropriate term in each situation.

From the point of view of the present study the distinction between the two terms "conception" and "experience" is of great importance because my aim is not to investigate the conceptual features of certain limited subject matter, but rather the sense-related features of experiencing learning holistically. Thus, according to what is discussed above, there remains no need for further argumentation for using the terms "experience" or "ways of experiencing" to denote my unit and object of investigation. I will work with Marton's (1996a) and Marton and Pong's (2005) guidance by applying the terms "experience" or "way of experiencing" throughout the study to denote the object of research.

The Knowledge Interest of the Phenomenographic Approach

Like other qualitative research approaches, the phenomenographic approach assumes that the kind of research that studies subjective knowledge is a valuable endeavour, and that within subjective knowledge, there is meaning and understanding that reflect various views of phenomena. These various views are judged to be fundamental to the way in which we act, understand, form our beliefs and experience our world. (Barnard, McCosker & Gerber 1999, 215.)

In phenomenography it is claimed that we cannot meaningfully talk about inexperienced reality. Consequently, it is argued that people's different ways of experiencing the surrounding world are all there is. Hence the researcher can compare different experiences with each other but what he/she is unable to do is to compare them with reality itself. (Uljens 1996, 112-113.) This brings in the fact that the view of knowledge taken in phenomenography is relational. It is created by human beings in relation to external reality (Svensson 1997, 165). Actually, experiencing something is relational in two senses. On the one hand it is relational in being a relation between the experiencer and the phenomenon (reality) and, on the other hand, it is relational in the sense that the same experiencer may experience the phenomenon in various ways in relation to varying situations (McKenzie 2003, 80). In connection with the present study a relational view of knowledge is discussed in more detail in Section 3.2.

According to the above line of reasoning it is essential from the point of view of the present study to note here that describing experience and ways of experiencing is not the same as describing a human being's mental representations, the "conceptual apparatus of the cognitivists", as Marton and Booth (1997, 113) put it. Whereas cognitivism is a theory of psychological processes, phenomenography is a theory of how to describe manifestations of human experience and qualitative differences between these. This simply means that thinking in the cognitivist sense is totally excluded from phenomenographic research approach. (Uljens 1996, 173.) Hence, in a phenomenographic sense "[t]hinking is either a fiction or an experience", as stated by Marton (1996a, 173). Marton likewise relies more on the statement "Cognose ergo sum" (I experience, therefore I am) than Descartes' original formulation "Cogito ergo sum" (I think, therefore I am) (ibid.).

5.2.2 Outcomes of the Phenomenographic Approach

The outcomes of the phenomenographic research approach are presented unambiguously by Marton (1997, 100) as consisting of categories of description and an outcome space. Essentially, the descriptive categories and the outcome space serve as tools to capture and communicate the features of the experiences or the phenomenon they represent (Bruce 1997, 87). Åkerlind (2005b) outlines the primary features of the outcomes of phenomenographic approach as follows:

> Outcomes are represented analytically as a number of qualitatively different meanings or ways of experiencing the phenomenon (called 'categories of description' to distinguish the empirically interpreted category from the hypothetical experience that it represents), but also including the structural relationships linking these different ways of experiencing. These relationships represent the structure of the 'outcome space', in terms of providing an elucidation of relations between different ways of experiencing the one phenomenon. (Åkerlind 2005b, 322)

Categories of Description

The categories of description are the researcher's way of expressing the different ways of experiencing the phenomenon. Therefore they do not refer directly to any mental reality. (Uljens 1996, 119.) According to Marton (1988, 181) the categories have four primary characteristics. They are relational in the sense that they deal with the subject-object relation of the experiences that they indicate. They are experiential in the sense that they are based on the experiences of research participants. They are content oriented in the sense that they focus on the meaning of the phenomenon under study to those who experience the phenomenon. And finally they are qualitative and descriptive in the sense that they are made visible through language. An individual category of description represents one way of experiencing the phenomenon (Cope 2000, 78).

Marton and Booth (1997, 125-126) have established three criteria for the quality of a set of categories of description. Firstly, each category should contribute something unique about a particular way of experiencing the phenomenon. Secondly, the categories have to be in a logical relationship with each other. That relationship is most often hierarchical in nature. This means that there should be "a series of increasingly complex subsets of the totality of the diverse ways of experiencing various phenomena" (ibid., 126). The idea of a categorisation system is illustrated by Marton (1986) below (the words in parenthesis are mine):

> ...each category is a potential part of a larger structure in which the category is related to other categories of description. It is a goal of phenomenography to discover the structural framework within which various categories of understanding [experience] exist. (Marton 1986, 34)

And thirdly, the categorisation system should include as few categories as is feasible and reasonable to capture the critical variation in the data. That is, it should be parsimonious (Marton & Booth 1997, 126).

Outcome Space

The ultimate aim of phenomenographic analysis is to constitute an outcome space representing the core aspects of the collective meanings or ways of experiencing the phenomenon among the sample group in a particular situation (Åkerlind 1999).

An outcome space is a diagrammatic representation of the logical relationships between experiences of the phenomenon (Bruce 1997, 87; Barnard, McCosker & Gerber 1999, 220). As defined by Marton and Booth (1997, 125), "[t]he complex of categories of description capturing the different ways of experiencing the phenomenon is the outcome space…it comprises distinct groupings of aspects of the phenomenon and the relationships between them." Each category of description forms part of a larger whole in which each one is related in the form of outcome space. Hence the portrayal of the logical relationship between categories of description in the form of outcome space is a representation of the phenomena in the same way as categories of description are representations of experiences. (Barnard, McCosker & Gerber 1999, 220; see also Marton 1994b, 29.)

Using the idea of new phenomenography and the anatomy of awareness the different aspects of the phenomenon discerned and held simultaneously in focal awareness are seen to constitute an outcome space of variation of the phenomenon (Marton & Fai 1999).

According to Laurillard (1993, 45; see also Järvinen & Järvinen 2000) there are three types of outcome spaces in which the relations between different categories may be viewed. The first is an inclusive, hierarchical, outcome space in which the categories further up the hierarchy include the previous or lower ones. The second type is an outcome space in which the different categories are related to the history of the participant's experience of the phenomenon. And the third is an outcome space which represents a developmental progression in the sense that the experiences represented by some category have more explanatory power that others, and thus may be seen as better than others. From the point of view of this study the outcome space is likely to be the first one but with weighty developmental elements.

When interpreting the outcomes of the phenomenographic approach, one should take into account that the descriptive categories and the outcome space aim to describe the variation in the key ways in which the experiences of the phenomenon differ. Hence, they are not thought to represent rich descriptions of the experiences themselves. Nor are they intended to describe individual differences in experience nor the full variation in experiencing a phenomenon (i.e. we always experience phenomena in a limited number of ways). (Prosser, Martin, Trigwell et al. 2005, 151.)

The essential features of phenomenographic approach are summarised in Table 3. These features have a significant impact, especially when collecting and analysing the data and interpreting the results. The features are elaborated below according to Åkerlind's (2005b, 6-8) taxonomy.

Table 3. *The distinguishing features of a phenomenographic research approach*

Distinguishing features	Explanations of features
Related, not independent meanings	Each meaning may be regarded as a fragment of human understanding of the whole phenomenon (Åkerlind 2005a, 6), ". . . the meaning of one bit derived from the meaning of and lending meaning to the rest" (Marton and Booth 1997, 124).
Awareness, not beliefs	A certain way of experiencing something is a way of being aware of it. Awareness is a relationship between subject and object. A person's awareness is the world as experienced by the person (Marton 1997, 97-98,108).
Context (situation) sensitive, not stable constructs	Our experience of anything is always embedded in a situation (Marton & Booth 1997, 96). Every situation has it own relevance structure. This means that the same individual may experience the same phenomenon differently under different circumstances (Åkerlind 2005a, 7).
Interpretive, not explanatory focus	The key aim of phenomenographic research is descriptive or interpretive rather than explanatory, i.e., to investigate what sort of differences in meaning and understanding occur across individuals rather than to attempt to explain or investigate causes of these differences (Åkerlind 2005a, 7-8).
Collective, not individual experience	The description is a description on a collective level (Marton & Booth 1997, 114). Although the research data involves collection of descriptions of individual experiences (as the collective view can only be accessed via individual views), the data analyses and research outcomes do not emphasise the experience of individual, but rather the collective experience of the sample group as a whole (Åkerlind 2005a, 8).
Stripped, not rich descriptions	"it is a stripped description... of differing ways of experiencing" (Marton & Booth 1997, 114). Therefore, rather than focusing on the endless variation inherent in the richness of individual experience, phenomenographic research focuses on identifying what is critical for distinguishing one way of experiencing from a qualitatively different way, in terms of the minimum features necessary for drawing such distinctions (Åkerlind 2005a, 8).

5.2.3 *Criticism of the Phenomenographic Approach*

> Clear methodological guidelines for phenomenography are lacking, as is a clarification of epistemological and ontological foundations and their consequences. **At the end of the day phenomenography appears to be a form of discourse analysis in which the relations of production of discourse and meaning designation are often simply ignored.** (Hasselgren and Beach 1998, 7)

As with most qualitative research, phenomenography has been subject to criticism regarding its principles and practices. My aim here is not to defend the chosen approach against this criticism but rather to tell the reader about the shortcomings attributed to the phenomenographic approach and to which the researchers have to be alert when conducting an investigation. Boulton-Lewis and Wills (2004) suggest that as long as the researcher is aware of these limitations, phenomenography is a powerful way of determining and describing how a specific group of people in a specific context experience a designated phenomenon.

The criticism of phenomenography can be categorised into two areas of concern. Firstly, phenomenography can be criticised similarly to other qualitative methodologies. The second type of criticism concerns how the phenomenographic method has been implemented. (Hales & Watkins 2004.) There has been debate particularly about the following issues: the phenomenographic approach itself (Giorgi 1999); the absence of published guidelines for conducting phenomenographic research, particularly the process of analysis (Entwistle 1997; Hasselgren and Beach 1998); lack of epistemological and ontological foundations of phenomenography (Hasselgren and Beach 1998); rigour and reliability of the results (Sandberg 1996, 1997; Richardson 1999); phenomenographic interviewing and the status of interview data (Francis 1993, 1996; Säljö 1996, 1997; Richardson 1999); entering into the life-world of the learner (Ashworth & Lucas 1998, 2000).

My intention here is not to scrutinise the shortcomings further, i.e., in isolation from their context; I rather favour elaborating them throughout the book in connection with the matters they address. There is, however, one complaint, voiced by Giorgi (1999), concerning the methodical and theoretical elements of phenomenography which, due to its fundamental nature, deserves to be mentioned here (the words in parenthesis are mine).

> ...when they [Marton & Boot 1997] write that phenomenography is not a method, but has methodical elements and that it is not a theory, but has theoretical elements, it is like having your cake and eating it, too. This gives phenomenographers complete license to be theoretical or not, or methodical or not, according to whichever position is most advantageous at the moment. This means that it does not meet the most rigorous demands of a scientific approach. For me, this reflects more an incompleteness of phenomenography rather than its ultimate stance. (Giorgi 1999)

Giorgi (1999) argues that there are some difficulties in determining what the parameters of phenomenography actually are. He sees it as problematic that phenomenographers "want to claim some methodical elements without being fully methodical and some theoretical status without being completely theoretical" (ibid.).

Åkerlind (2005a, 322) has recently observed that while methodological debates and critiques have become more common, these discussions fail to take into account accepted variations in phenomenographic practices. Åkerlind supposes that the relative lack of publications of phenomenographic methodology has led to criticism which may be founded on misinterpretations of the nature of the phenomenographic research approach. Another source of misunderstandings, as noted by Åkerlind, may be the fact that phenomenographic contributions to the research literature are often assessed by journal reviewers without a clear awareness of the unique methodological requirements of the approach.

From the perspective of the present study the criticism above poses many threats at every level of the research. Therefore, instead of being ignored or belittled, they are taken seriously by the present researcher to diminish their undesired consequences.

The preceding sections of this chapter have described the major assumptions associated with phenomenographic research approach in general terms, rather than placing emphasis on the detailed requirements that stem from the present research. The methodological issues related particularly to this study will be discussed in the next chapter (6) in relation to the implementation of the research.

6 IMPLEMENTATION OF THE RESEARCH

This chapter describes the research methods used in the present research; the selection of participants and the methods of data collection as well as steps taken when analysing that data. The chapter also evaluates the data gathering procedures and the quality of the data obtained. This description is in accordance with the principles of qualitative and interpretative research methodology used in my research, where the truth constellation involves, above all, the researcher making transparent (e.g. Sandberg 2005, 59) how he/she has dealt with his/her intentional relation to the lived experience under investigation.

6.1 Selection of Participants

In this section I will discuss the sampling strategy, the criteria for selecting the participants and introduce those characteristics of the participants that are relevant for the purpose of the research. The essential criteria for choosing the participants for the present type of research include first and foremost that these individuals have experienced the phenomenon that the research is interested in, are keen on exploring that phenomenon and are willing to participate in the research (see e.g. Moustakas 1994, 107). When designing the selection of participants I tried to take these essential criteria into account.

I adopted a purposeful sampling strategy (see e.g. Patton 2002, 243), as is customary in phenomenographic research, for both maximum variation sampling and criterion sampling type. Maximum variation sampling includes "purposefully picking a wide range of cases to get variation on dimensions of interest" and criterion sampling "[p]icking all cases that meet some criterion" (ibid.). Given that my research question arose from an interest in variation in how adult learners experienced their learning in the university setting, the sample was consequently selected with the purpose of highlighting such variation. The idea behind purposeful sampling strategy is well documented by Merriam (1988) (though using the term purposive):

> Purposive sampling is based on the assumption that one wants to discover, understand, gain insight; therefore one needs to select a sample from which one can learn most. (Merriam 1988, 48)

To put it more clearly, purposeful sampling strategy involves seeking maximum diversity in those characteristics considered most important to the research questions, whereas random probability sampling strategy seeks proportional representativeness of the whole population (e.g. Patton 2002, 243).

Considering the selection of participants Ashworth and Lucas (2000, 301), point out that it should avoid assumptions about the nature of the phenomenon held by particular types of individuals. However, "[s]uch assumptions should be identified and put aside, in the sense of acknowledging them and being aware of the possibility that they are false" (Ashworth & Lucas 2000, 302). When selecting research participants for a phenomenographic research the researcher should therefore have criteria related to the variation in the issue of interest in mind, but he/she should not take a particular kind of variation for granted in advance.

When choosing the participants I tried to involve students of different status (under- and postgraduate), age, gender, disciplinary background, areas of subject orientation as well as work background. This is based on a phenomenographic idea that the context in which one exists is of value to the experiences one has (see e.g. Case 2000, 100).

A total of 71 TUKEVA students participated in the research (see Tables 4 and 5). The core participants were a group of 18 interviewees while a further 53 people provided supplementary data in written form. The sample involved students from four different universities and five different university units. The students came from three main disciplinary areas; education, economics and technology. Within economics there were three different subjects and within technology four. The participants were represented in all of these.

The core sample group (interview) included 13 females and 5 males and a supplementary sample group (written data) 39 females and 14 males. The males' samples were smaller than females' because the proportion of males among the students was smaller in general. The age of the participants varied between 27 and 58 years, the average age being approximately 44 years.

The participants had in common their professional field, relating to adult vocational education, and their ongoing studies in TUKEVA. As a whole the students selected had a range of work experience, particularly in the field of adult education. They also had extensive study experiences, including university level, which were, to some degree, relevant to their recent studies in TUKEVA. It can be said that each student had a unique context for his/her studies in terms of the relevant academic experience as well as physical and social environments. (cf. Booth & Hulten 2003, 66.)

To sum up, the participants were chosen to ensure that maximum variation was obtained from within the selected context. This strategy has been labelled purposeful sampling. Although details of the individuals are not for ethical reasons provided here, information about the characteristics of the participants, their universities, disciplines, degrees and genders, are presented below in Tables 4 and 5.

Table 4. *University, degree, discipline and gender backgrounds of interviewees*

University	Degree	Discipline	Number of males	Number of females
University of Jyväskylä	B.Sc. (Econ.)	Economics		3
University of Jyväskylä	M.Sc. (Econ.)	Economics		3
University of Tampere	B.A. (Educ.)	Education		2
University of Tampere	M.A. (Educ.)	Education	1	1
University of Tampere	Lic.Educ.	Education		2
Tampere University of Technology, Edutech	M.Sc. (Eng.)	Engineering	2	
Tampere University of Technology, Edupoint	M.Sc. (Eng.)	Engineering	1	1
Helsinki University of Technology, Lahti Center	M.Sc. (Eng.)	Engineering	1	1
Total number of interviewees (18)			5	13

Table 5. *University, degree, discipline and gender backgrounds of participants of written accounts*

University	Degree	Discipline	Number of males	Number of females
University of Jyväskylä	B.Sc. (Econ.)	Economics		13
University of Jyväskylä	M.Sc. (Econ)	Economics	1	3
University of Tampere	B.A. (Educ.)	Education	5	13
University of Tampere	M.A. (Educ.)	Education	8	10
Total number of participants (53)			14	39

All in all, 108 students were asked to participate in the research. Finally 71 students were involved in it.

6.2 Methods of Data Collection

In this section I will discuss the methods employed when gathering the data for the research. Determining data collection methods depends on the nature of the phenomenon and purpose of the research; what kind of data is needed to fulfil that purpose, to answer the questions posed by the researcher. Since the purpose of this research was to describe adult learners' experiences of their learning (experience is assumed to be qualitative in nature), an essential part of the methodology was to identify a method (or methods) to enable learners to make explicit those experiences of learning, i.e. to determine the data gathering technique(s).

Phenomenographic data collection aims to capture a pool of meanings that express the varying ways in which a particular phenomenon is experienced within the sample group (Berglund 2005, 62). This second order perspective, behind the phenomenographic approach, has implications for the data collection techniques used (e.g. Cope 2000, 79). In phenomenographic research the researcher does not attempt to describe what reality is like (first order perspective) but how it is experienced and described by the people who experience it (second order perspective). Therefore, from the perspective of this research, the source of the data must be the learners themselves (see e.g. Booth 2001, 172). A prerequisite for the data gathering procedure in phenomenographic research, no matter which technique, is first and foremost, that it should allow the participants to "express their own way of structuring the aspects of reality they are relating to" (Johansson, Marton & Svensson 1985, 252).

In this research semi-structured interviews and accounts written in participants' own words were used as the means of gathering data on the experiences of learning. The interviews were used as primary data (as is customary in phenomenographic research) and the written accounts as a supplementary data to ensure the validity and reliability of the research. Based on my knowledge, achieved through literature, as well as my practical experience as a researcher, I assume that these methods should adhere to the principles of a phenomenographic study of learning (the principles are discussed above and in several parts of this report). The reason for using interviews as the core data collection method has to do with the structure of awareness. It includes an idea that "[t]he more it is possible to make things that are unathematised and implicit into objects of reflection and hence thematised and explicit, the more fully can awareness be explored" (Marton 1997, 99). It is thought that an interview is the appropriate method for that purpose. Thus, while the interviews generated my primary data, the fundamental features of the manner of data collection are described next. After that, I will proceed to demonstrate how the interviews were carried out. And finally, at the end of this section, the written data collection procedures will be explained.

6.2.1 Conducting Interviews

At a general level, as concluded by Kvale (1996, 1) "the qualitative research interview attempts to understand the world from the subject's point of view, to unfold the meaning of peoples' experiences, to uncover their lived world ..." What is stated by Kvale (ibid.) accords well with the aims of my data gathering. In phenomenographic research in particular, while collecting data the researcher wishes "to bring to light the ways in which the people being studied experience the phenomenon of interest" (Marton & Booth 1997, 129). The most usual way of bringing people's experiences to light in phenomenographic studies is through semi-structured interviews (see e.g. Marton & Booth 1997, 132; Cope 2000, 91; Berglund 2005, 62).

Marton (1997, 99) restricts the nature of a phenomenographic interview to an interviewer-interviewee exploration of the phenomenon under research as seen by the interviewee. The interview consists of productive interactions in which the data is constituted by the interviewee and interviewer when negotiating on the phenomenon (Dortins 2002, 209). The researcher intends to focus the interviewees' awareness towards the phenomenon (here the phenomenon of learning) and bring them to reflect on it (McKenzey 2003, 85) in such a way that the interviewee can describe the ways in which he/she experiences the phenomenon (Berglund 2005, 62). Concerning interviewees' reflection (also called meta-awareness) Marton et al. (1997) note that

> Sometimes such reflection occurs spontaneously, and sometimes the interviewer and the interviewee have to work together to reach the required state...(Marton & Booth 1997, 130)

The above means that the awareness of experience is tapped through the interviewee's reflection and description (e.g. Francis 1993, 70). The quote below from Marton (1994a), captures the salient features of a phenomenographic interview very well (the italics are mine).

> The interview has to be *carried out as a dialogue*; it should facilitate the thematisation of aspect of the subject's experience not previously thematised. The experiences, understandings, are *jointly constituted by interviewer and interviewee*. These experiences, understandings, are neither there prior to the interview, ready to be "read off", nor are they only situational social constructions. They are *aspects of the subject's awareness* that change *from being unreflected to being reflected*. (Marton 1994a, 4427)

When conducting the interviews, I was alert to what had been said on the topic by several authors of phenomenographic research but I certainly adapted their ideas for the purpose of my own research and the phenomena of interest.

In this research a total of 18 individual interviews were conducted by the present author when acquiring data on the participants' learning experiences on the TUKEVA programme. I carried out the interviews between May and September 2002. They were semi-structured face-to-face interviews except for one which, due the interviewee's family situation, was organised by phone. However, this interview followed the same pattern as all the other interviews.

Some weeks before the interviews took place, I contacted the potential participants (purposive sampling of maximum variation sampling type is discussed in Section 6.1) by phone in order to ascertain their willingness to contribute to the research by participating in the interview. If I did not reach them by phone, I used e-mail as the secondary approach.

During the phone calls I first introduced myself, if I did not already know them. As became evident in Section 2.2, some of the participants knew me prior to the interviews. In addition, I explained to them the purpose of the research, and their potential role in it was as well outlined. The goal of the interview and the way it would be conducted were also explained. It is of great importance to tell the participants beforehand about the purpose of the research and interview, as recommended by Ashworth and Lucas (2000, 299), "the research interviews have to be introduced to the interviewee as being about something… [t]he researcher and researched must begin with some kind of superficially shared topic, verbalised in terms which they both recognise as meaningful."

No one refused my invitation to attend the interview and they were instead very keen to contribute to the research. Thereafter we jointly outlined potential times and dates for the discussions at the participants' convenience.

Eight interviews were conducted in the offices of the participants and three in my own office. Six interviews took place in a university meeting room, and, as mentioned earlier, one interview was carried out by phone, the interviewee being at home and the researcher in her office. All interviews were carried out during the official working hours of both parties.

As is essential, the interviews took place in strict privacy. That is, apart from the researcher and the participant no one else was present in the room when the interview took place. In addition, all possible interruptions and other disturbances were avoided, for instance, by diverting phonecalls and shutting the door. In addition, "do not disturb" sign was placed on the outside of the door.

At the start of each interview I recapitulated to the interviewee the purpose of my research and explained the goal of the interview: to get an impression of the participant's ways of experiencing their learning in TUKEVA-programme. It was explained that the interview would flexibly follow a semi-structured format. Ethical issues and confidentiality were also discussed and I assured the participants that they would remain anonymous. I furthermore explained that they would be given time to reflect on their experiences. That is in line with Sjöström and Dahlberg's (2002, 341) advice that the interview is open and that the interviewee is permitted to think aloud, to hesitate, and even take a break if necessary. The participants were also advised that the interview would be recorded on tape. (e.g. Moustakas 1994, 107). The interviewees expressed no resistance to such documentation with regard to their spoken accounts.

In order to create a good rapport and create a relaxed and trusting atmosphere for an effective interview, small talk and other chat were shared between the researcher and participant prior to interviewing. When interviewing, I as a general rule avoided an authoritative style and instead used a conversational style to encourage the participants to talk more freely about their experiences. It is also worth mentioning here that in the course of interviewing I did not make any written notes, but just concentrated on the conversational interaction with the participant.

A phenomenographic type of interview should neither have too many questions formulated beforehand, nor should there be too many details determined beforehand, as Marton (1994a, 4427; 1997, 99) advices. Booth (1992) also places emphasis on the same matter by noting that

> ...having a small number of predetermined questions which deliberately approach the phenomenon from a variety of directions and thus increase the chances of a full exploration... (Booth 1992, 59-60)

My interview included six topics formulated in advance to elicit the participants' ways of experiencing their learning. I did not provide the interviewees with any written material of those questions. The themes were:

1. Describe your intentions to start studying on the TUKEVA programme. What made you begin studying?
2. Describe what kind of goals you had for your studies?
3. Describe your experiences of being a TUKEVA student. What has it been like so far?
4. Describe things that have fostered and/or inhibited your studying.

5. Describe your ways of experiencing learning on the TUKEVA programme.
6. Describe the meaning the studies have to you.

Berglund (2005, 62) advices the researcher to begin an interview with a cluster of open questions about what he/she wants to learn from the interviewee. Sjöström and Dahlgen (2002, 341) recommend a few opening questions as well. When starting an interview, the main thing, however, is that the researcher's opening words encourage the participant to begin his/her own search for experiences of interest. When it came to the beginnings of my interviews, I undertook them smoothly with questions concerning the respondents' learning history in TUKEVA; for how long they had been studying on the TUKEVA programme and what kind of intentions and aims they had behind their studies (questions 1 and 2). With those topics I intended to learn something about the participants' learning paths in TUKEVA as well as their overall motives and aims in their studies.

The rule that one should not make too many questions at the start of the session is based on the idea that most questions should actually follow from what the interviewee says. This implies that the researcher has a crucial task when interviewing. He/she has to catch the phenomenon as experienced by the interviewee and to explore it jointly and as exhaustively as possible (see e.g. Marton 1994a, 4427; 1997, 99).

After the above-described opening questions, I continued the interviewing by posing questions related to the participants' learning experiences more generally. Marton and Booth (1997, 132) recommend that attempts should be made to vary the focus of the interviewees' awareness and reflection (or meta-awareness) around the aspects of interest. We therefore talked about what it had been like to study in TUKEVA (question 3) and the possible fostering factors as well as inhibitors they had faced in the course of their studies (question 4). The information that I got through that discussion formed an important background needed when delving deeper into the participants' lived learning experiences (questions 5 and 6). This knowledge also helped me in my handling of the key issue of interest: the way of experiencing learning. This part of the interview generally followed the next form.

Can you describe what you experience you have learned in these couple of years?

I think I've learned a kind of wide outlook on working life, vocational education and life in general. In a sense my perspective has expanded quite a lot. Actually I don't remember so much of the details but some bigger insights. Or I've had big insights as an individual person. Like is this the way that something is? I think that's the best thing I've had in there. I can't necessarily even list theories, I've seen and heard a lot of them but... perhaps regarding learning I have begun to see more entities than details. That means my habit was to try to learn the main points but now I begin to see these things...first of all they're not black and white and then the fact that they are a kind of entities. So I think studying has developed a certain kind of way of thinking.

The interviews were brought to a close when both parties felt that all aspects of the participant's experiences of learning in TUKEVA had been explored. The closing question was typically expressed in the form of "Is there anything else you want to tell me about your experiencing on the TUKEVA programme?" On the completion of the interview I expressed my gratitude for the participant's contribution to the knowledge, crucial for the research and practice.

In line with phenomenographic principles the interview situations resembled, on a general level, dynamic discussions more than highly structured interviews. Naturally, the course of the different interviews varied somewhat due to their exploratory (e.g. Cope 2004) and dialogical (e.g. Marton & Booth 1997) nature and relationship to the ideas expressed by the interviewee.

In the course of the interviews, follow-up questions were presented when thought relevant. They were mainly raised on occasions when I wanted to ensure that I had understood the interviewees' expressions in the same way as they had intended them (see e.g. Kvale 1996, 31). Other occasions when I used follow-up questions included those when I encouraged the participants to reflect further on a topic or checked whether the participant presented his/her real experiences realistically (i.e. was not trying to fool me). There is a concern in the phenomenographic interview about how not to manipulate (lead, put interviewer's words into the mouth of interviewee) the participant with the follow-up questions (see e.g. Francis 1996). Hence, good care should be taken to avoid leading questions (Francis 1993, 70; 1996, 38-39). As a solution, it is suggested that only such terms should be used that are borrowed from the interviewee's own utterances (e.g. Cope 2002). Therefore, considerable emphasis must be put on how the participants articulate their views on the issue at hand (Sjöström and Dahlgren 2002, 339).

Overall, when articulating participant's ideas back to him/her I tried to adjust my choice of words to use the terms the interviewees used in their own expressions. In order not to lead the participants, I also resisted temptations to speak aloud (or even think) about my own points of view or to comment about the issues taken up by the interviewees. It is also important to note here that a person's experiences can never be right or wrong. Therefore the researcher should avoid all assessment of the participant's expressions of their experiences (Sjöström and Dahlberg 2002, 341).

It is just as important to avoid generating assumptions that go beyond the participant's lived experience. Sandberg (2005, 60) warns about this danger by assuming that "as soon as the researchers surpass what is given in their experience, they begin to explain and use their arsenal of theories and models, which essentially are outside what is lived experience." I therefore tried to ignore my own prior knowledge and experiences of learning and ensure that my interpretations were based on participants' learning experiences and not my own.

The above is called a process of epoché (Moustakas 1994, 116). The aim of the epoché is to ensure that the researcher sets aside his/her theories or prejudice (Sandberg 2005, 60), and that they do not colour or influence (Moustakas 1994, 116) his/her interpretations of the experience. The epoché does not, however, mean that the researcher should bracket or be even capable of bracketing all his/her previous knowledge and experiences (Sandberg 2005, 60 referring to Giorgi 1990). This is impossible, because in reality we always interpret things within the framework of our lived experience (this is also the idea behind phenomenography), i.e., we are prisoners of our own past (biography). The point behind the epoché is, as expressed by Giorgi (1990, 71), that the researcher brackets the knowledge relevant to the issue at hand.

After carrying out twelve interviews, it appeared that the interviewees' utterances were starting to resemble each other. However, I interviewed six more participants, as planned, to ensure that no new ways of experiencing learning emerged. When it became apparent that no new statements were being generated, there was no need for further interviews. With the participants' consent, which they all willingly gave, these interviews were then used as empirical data in the present research (see e.g. Moustakas 1994, 107).

The duration of the taped interviews was usually a little over one hour, the shortest taking about 45 minutes and the longest nearly two hours; the total duration being approximately 25 hours. The transcript data consists of 243 pages (A4), typed with the spacing of 1.5, with left and right marginal both set at 1.5 centimetres.

6.2.2 Collecting Written Data

Written accounts were used as supplementary data in the present research. That is, as a triangulation method to ensure the validity and reliability of the research. With regard to written data Bruce (1997), for example, sees it as well-suited for phenomenographic research. It is, however, important that the written data method used is of the open answer type rather than being limited in advance by the researcher (Cope 2000, 79). This is because phenomenographic research essentially prefers openness in data gathering.

Written accounts are parallel to some types of personal diaries. They refer to individuals' written first person accounts of the whole or parts of their lives or their reflections on a specific event or topic (Taylor & Bodgan 1984, 113). From the perspective of the present research the parts of participants' lives and the specific events of their reflections were the experiencing learning on the TUKEVA programme.

Comparing the spoken and written methods used for data collection in this research, some differences between them can be observed. Kroksmark (2006 in press, 5-6), for instance, suggests that in written text several dimensions are lost compared with the spoken word. According to him (ibid.), written language is never as spontaneous as speech. It is planned and structured and follows rules established beforehand. It is also allowed to develop and finish without the researcher's interruptions. Whereas spoken language in interviews is tied to the shared ongoing situations, the written text could have been written at several points in time by someone unknown to the researcher, whom he/she has never met or is ever going to meet (Kroksmark 2006 in press, 5-6.), as was the case in the present research.

The sample group for the written accounts method consisted of all the TUKEVA university students that had already taken their degrees or were about to graduate. Information on these students was based on the lists provided for the present researcher by the universities organising the TUKEVA studies.

The fact that the written accounts were collected from learners close to or after graduation means that the accounts covered their whole learning period on the TUKEVA programme; from the very beginning of their studies until the very end. Thus, when writing their accounts, the learners had approximately three to four years of studies behind them.

The written data was gathered in two phases, depending on the time of the graduation. The first phase was conducted between April and August 2003 (29 students) and the second between May and July 2004 (61 students). Prior to sending the written account forms to the students, permission to do so was requested by e-mail. The same e-mail also contained the basic information about the research. No one declined to take part in the research and the students were therefore sent an e-mail with the following instructions.

> Following the topics given, you should freely reflect on your own TUKEVA experiences. Because the topics have no right or wrong answers, you should describe your thoughts freely. I will not pay attention to the linguistic or structural form of your writing. The most important thing is that you describe your TUKEVA experiences as fully as possible. In addition to the topics given, there is also room for your own themes, should you have something that you would like to write about.

Attached to this e-mail was a form with open-ended questions. The form included five questions, of which the following three were particularly relevant to the present research.

1. What kind of experiences have you had in your studies on the TUKEVA programme?
2. What do you feel you have learnt when studying on the TUKEVA programme?
3. What kind of meaning do the TUKEVA studies have for you, as a whole?

I gave the students about one month to reflect on their experiences and write them down for me. A reminder letter was sent by e-mail to those students who had not replied within that time limit. In spite of this reminder, 37 students never returned their accounts, the most commonly reported reason being lack of time.

Through the written accounts I received data from 53 individuals, written in their own words and without any manipulation or involvement on my part. Just like the interviews, the written questions also included some follow-up questions. But in this case it was more up to the participant him/herself to answer or not to answer them. Each person wrote a paragraph of between nine and hundreds words in response to the 5 questions. The total number of single-spaced pages (A4) of written accounts was 120.

6.3 Evaluation of the Data Gathering Procedures and the Data

The results of research are based on the gathered data. For that reason it is crucial that the data be of good quality, i.e. it has worth and it is genuine in relation to the phenomena under investigation. Before starting to analyse my data, I therefore evaluate what kind of data gathering procedures I have used and what kind data I have gathered.

From the perspective of the present research, there are a huge number of details concerning the data gathering process and data obtained through that process that can be evaluated. However, the space available does not allow me to discuss all of them (it might also be quite exhausting from the point of view of the reader). I will therefore restrict my evaluation to concern five main areas, viewing them as the most crucial with regard to the nature (phenomenographic research) and purpose (explore the adult learners' ways of experiencing their learning and describe the variation in different ways of experiencing learning) of the present research. The areas to be evaluated here are: the selection of the participants, data collection methods, themes (questions) used in acquiring the data, the context of data gathering and the interviewer's role. These topics are not mutually exclusive, although they are described below one at a time, but inter-related. I will first approach them at a general level, and then at the end of this section, in Table 6, I will focus on them, providing examples of practices applied.

My first concern is about the relevancy of the selection of the participants. As far as the number of participants is concerned, Sandberg's (1994, 72) opinion is that it should be sufficient to yield adequately rich descriptions of the varying experiences, and that approximately twenty participants will achieve this. In my research eighteen participants contributed to the core data, i.e. by participating in the interviews, while a further fifty three participants provided supplementary data in written form. This is therefore in accordance with Sandberg's recommendation above.

The aim of a phenomenographic data gathering procedure is to obtain descriptions of a broad range of experiences. Therefore, it is important to evaluate here whether there were variations in the selected participants' experiences of learning. As noted by Ashworth and Lucas (2000, 302), selecting participants who seem intuitively likely to have different experiences of the phenomenon assumed, is valuable. However, this kind of operation is built on the premise of intuitive likelihood and hence may also be false (ibid.). My assumption was that selecting participants deliberately, according to certain criteria (see Section 6.1), would allow me to obtain such data that involves variation with regard to the participants' learning experiences on the TUKEVA programme. At first glance (in phenomenographic interviews the analysis starts simultaneously with the data collection) the data obtained seems to meet the requirements of variation in experiences, but the final analysis will ultimately reveal whether this is so.

It is, however, not enough that the "right" participants are involved in the research. That is, participants with a variety of experiences of the phenomenon in question. In addition to this, these participants must have the motivation (see e.g. Sjöström & Dahlgren 2002, 341) to talk about their experiences. Hence, my next concern is whether the participants were motivated to talk about their experiences of learning. Having elicited participants' willingness to take part in the research and they not having declined my invitation, I can conclude that they were all motivated to talk about their experiences. Before ascertaining their willingness, I had, of course, informed them about the purpose of my research as well as their role in it (to recount their experiences of learning on the TUKEVA programme).

Säljö (1997, 178) comments that, as "we have access to nothing but what people communicate…" the researcher "…should be extremely cautious of considering this as indicating a way of experiencing rather than as, for instance, a way of talking." This comment leads to a question of how the participants spoke about their experiences. Did they tell me their real experiences?

Sandberg (2005, 56 referring to Alvesson 2003), for example, has observed that the participants, as a rule, do not describe their experiences in an undistorted way, but in a way that is mediated via several factors, for example, moral storytelling, social codes and cultural scripts. The participants may also attempt, as Säljö (1997, 177) supposes, "…to fulfil their communicative obligations when being asked a question or wish not to lose face when confronted with an abstract and maybe difficult question." To a certain extent, I do agree with what is said above. Undoubtedly, the researcher has to be alert to such pitfalls, and he/she must endeavour to eliminate them, but at the same time he/she has to trust the accounts of the participants. Otherwise there will be no rationale for collecting individuals' written or spoken data for use in scientific research. The researcher is able to test the participants' accounts (their consistency), for instance, by means of various kinds of follow-up questions (which will be discussed further later on) as I did to diminish the effects of mediative factors.

When describing an ideal method for a phenomenographic research, Ashworth and Lucas (2000, 302) conclude that it is "founded on as open a technique for eliciting experience as possible." With regard to Ashworth and Lucas' principle above I will elaborate whether it was possible to reach students' different ways of experiencing learning with the data gathering methods used in the research. That is, if the interviews and written accounts were the correct methods for generating the data for my phenomenographic research.

I acknowledge that both those methods have shortcomings. Regarding phenomenographic interview, Sjöström and Dahlgren (2002, 341) list two problems. The first concerns the participants' motivation for participating in an interview. That matter has already been discussed above. The second concern relates to the interviewer's understanding of the interviewee's utterances. In order to be able to formulate further questions, the interviewer is forced to interpret what the interviewee is saying on the spot and therefore needs a quick and correct understanding (e.g. Kvale 1996, 147). As noted by Sjöström and Dahlgren (2002, 341), "any misunderstanding in this respect may jeopardize the quality of the interview data."

Kroksmark (2006 in press, 16-17) pays attention to the same issue, but also to the role of the interviewee. He (ibid.) sees the shortcomings of an interview being as embedded in the moments: in on-going moments "the interviewee has to weight his words on the golden scales, find the right tracks. Not too little; not too much. There is no room for analysis or distance. What is said is said here and now, in an on-going state..." (ibid.).

The other data collection method used in the research was that of written account. This method also has its weaknesses. Ashworth and Lucas (2000, 302), for example, have conceded that, whereas written data gathering allows the researcher to expand the research to more participants, it produces accounts that are limited in scope and difficult to pinpoint within the participant's lived experience.

I largely agree with the statements of several authors given above, on the shortcomings of the methods used in the present research. Hence, to overcome them, I used both spoken and written techniques so that they complement each other, i.e. as a triangulation of methods. Although both methods have their individual shortcomings, they also have several benefits with regard to phenomenographic data collection. An interview allows the researcher to focus on the participant's reflection on the phenomenon of interest and thereby produce accurate data for the purpose of the research. On the other hand, the written account method gives the participant an opportunity to take time to identify his/her experiences, and to reflect on them, thus enabling the generation of valid data.

My next concern relates to the themes (questions) used in the interviews and written account forms. Was it possible to access the students' different ways of experiencing learning (the purpose of the research) with these questions (predetermined and follow-up)? That is, were the questions appropriate to the purpose of the research?

When posing the questions, the starting point is, as also recommended by Ashworth and Lucas (2000, 302), that they should not be based on the researcher's own perception of the nature of the phenomenon, but should come into being out of a pure interest to bring the participants' experiences to light. In other words, the questions should compel the researcher to put aside his/her own assumptions (epoché) and instead encourage the participants to take their own reflective orientation towards the matters at hand. I concur with this idea, but at the same time I wish to point out that the questions should clearly be based on the purpose of the research and they should focus on the matter of interest, which originates in the initiative of the researcher. That is to say, that whereas the participant has authority over his/her experiences, the researcher has authority over the matter of what the research is about and what is relevant to it.

The pre-determined questions (see Sections 6.2.1 and 6.2.2) that I used in my both spoken and written methods for data gathering were open and indirect in style. This allowed the participants room and flexibility to identify their own experiences and reflect on them, and also opportunity to express these experiences in a style familiar to them. On the other hand, as already stated as essential, the questions were specific enough to focus the participants' reflection on the issues that interested me.

Regarding the follow-up questions, I used them carefully, posing them perhaps rather too seldom. When reading the transcribed texts I sometimes regretted not having pursued something that might have been noteworthy. I tried to avoid falling into the trap of what Francis (1993, 69; 1996) calls leading prompts, which I think, can most be embedded in the follow-up questions. Francis assumes that leading prompts will lead to self-fulfilling prophecies via behaviour confirmation (ibid.), hence making the participant express him/herself in an invalid manner.

My next concern relates to the context of the data gathering; whether it was relevant to produce data from the point of view of my research interest. Regarding the term context, it is understood here as being parallel (see also Adawi, Berglund et al. 2002, 82; Berglund 2005, 55) to the term situation and relating to the term situationality (see Section 3.4 on Rauhala's situationality). Marton and Booth (1997, 83) propose that "[w]e cannot separate our understanding of the situation of the phenomena that lend sense to the situation" and "…we are aware of the phenomena from the point of view of the particular situation." The same idea is also expressed by Berglund (2005, 58), "[t]he object of research is embedded in a context, and this context can be said to lend meaning to the object." As becomes apparent from these quotations, the phenomenon is experienced in its context. Through that interaction the context of the data gathering affects the quality of the data.

In this research there were at least three kinds of contexts; the first being the TUKEVA context, from which the experiences of learning were drawn, and the others being the contexts of the data gathering (contexts of interviews and written accounts), in which those experiences were expressed. Hence the TUKEVA context falls outside the topic of this section and as it has already been described in Section 2.1, it is not discussed here. With regard to the context of data collection Adawi et al. (2002, 85) argue that the central factors in phenomenographic research are the preparations made in order to create a successful context. Because the details of my preparations are given in Section 6.2.1, they are not repeated here.

When writing their written accounts, the participants had individual contexts of their own beyond the researcher's reach. This is quite the opposite situation compared to the context of interviewing, where the interviewer plays a significant role in constructing the context. As Clandinin and Connelly (1994, 420) point out, the way the interviewer acts, questions, and answers in the interview shapes the relationship between the interviewer and the interviewee and affects the way participants express themselves and recount their experiences.

Therefore, basing the research on interviews, as I did in the present research, draws attention to the competence of the interviewer. Did I, as an interviewer, have the competence to conduct an interview? Ashworth and Lucas (2000, 303) assert that the researchers' interviewing skills should be subject to ongoing review. Kvale (1996, 147), for his part, suggests that a "good interviewer is an expert in the topic of the interview as well as in human interaction." In addition to these competences Kroksmark (2006 in press, 16-17) lists such requirements for an interviewer as great self assurance, knowledge about others, a certain maturity as a person and researcher, and a tangible presence.

Whether I fulfilled all these requirements becomes largely apparent in Section 2.2, where I described myself. The interviews were in no way perfect, but it can be argued here that I managed to collect data that has worth and is genuine in relation to the phenomenon under investigation.

To summarise, the essential questions related to the evaluation of the data gathering procedures and the quality of the data are presented in Table 6 with empirical examples from my practices.

Table 6. *Summary of the evaluation of the data gathering procedures and the data*

Objects of evaluation	General concern	Particular concern	Effects on data	Examples of practices
Participants	Was the selection of participants relevant?	Did the participants have variations in their experiences of learning?	Worth of data	The participants interviewed were chosen purposefully (maximum variation, sampling type) to represent a cross-section (gender, discipline, degree level) of all TUKEVA students.
				The participants who wrote their accounts were chosen purposefully (criterion sampling type) from all graduated TUKEVA students.
		Were the participants motivated to attend the interview / write written accounts and describe their experiences of learning?	Worth of data	The participants' willingness to attend the interview and talk about their learning experiences was ascertained in advance by phone or e-mail and in the course of the interview by observation.
				The participants' willingness to write an account of their learning experiences was ascertained in advance by e-mail. No manipulation in either method was used to motivate the participants.
		Did the participants present their real experiences in the interviews and written accounts?	Worth and genuineness of data	Follow-up questions were used to check the cohesiveness of the participants' expressions.
Methods	Was it possible to reach the learners' different ways of experiencing learning with the data collection methods used?	Were the interviews and written accounts accurate methods for the purpose of this phenomenographic study?	Worth of data	Both methods allowed participants focused but free reflection on their experiences in relation to their learning in TUKEVA.
Themes and questions	Was it possible to reach the learners' different ways of experiencing learning with the aid of the themes used in interviews and questions used in written accounts?	Were the themes appropriate to the purpose of the study?	Genuineness of data	The themes (questions) in both data collection methods were designed to stick to the purpose of the study, and with the aim of revealing the phenomenon under investigation, i.e. ways of experiencing learning.
		Were the themes related to the same issues for the researcher and the research participants?	Genuineness of data	The themes were introduced in common everyday language instead of the special vocabulary of a discipline. The understanding of the themes was ensured with follow-up questions.

Context	Was the context (situation) of data gathering relevant?	Did the space and time of data gathering allow the participants time for reflection on their learning experiences?	Genuineness of data	The interviews took place at a mutually agreed time and place convenient for the participants. Privacy was assured and interruptions were eliminated. The written answers allowed flexibility regarding context; time and space to reflect.
Interviewer	Did I have, as the interviewer, the competence to interview?	When interviewing, did I support (rather than obstruct) participants' reflections on their learning experiences?	Genuineness of data (interview)	The interviews were carried out in a conversational manner in order to encourage participants to reflect on their learning experiences.
		Did I, in an on-going process, correctly understand what the participants were saying (the meaning of the participants' words)?	Genuineness of data (interview)	Follow-up questions were used in order to check understanding with regard to students' expressions.

The quality of the analysis is dependent on the quality of the data gathered. As the data has now been evaluated, I can proceed by describing how the data was analysed.

6.4 Data Analysis

This section describes the steps taken when analysing my empirical data phenomenographically. The overall purpose of qualitative analysis is to bring meaning, structure, and order to data (Anfara & Brown 2001, 12). With respect particularly to phenomenography, the aim of the analysis is to yield descriptive categories of the qualitative variation in the experience of the phenomenon found in the empirical data (Sandberg 1997, 28). Consequently, since the phenomenon in this research was the learning experiences of adult learners, the aim of my analysis was to yield descriptive categories of these. In what follows, I will first briefly describe phenomenographic analysis at a level of general principles and then provide a concrete description of my own practices.

Actually (as mentioned in Section 6.2), the analysis already starts in the course of the data collection and continues in a more focused form from there on. In general, a phenomenographic analysis consists of two stages. The first concentrates on identifying and describing the experiences in terms of their meanings (referential aspects) and the second concentrates on identifying the structural aspects of those meanings (Marton & Pong 2005, 337; Åkerlind 2005a, 324). The process of analysis is strongly iterative and comparative in nature. It includes repetitive organisation and reorganisation of the data and comparison between the data and the emerging categories, as well as between the categories themselves. (Åkerlind 2005a, 321.) This iteration is well captured by Marton (1986, 42), "…[the] categories are tested against the data, adjusted, retested, and adjusted again".

As an individual may express a number of ways of experiencing the phenomenon, he/she is not the unit of analysis (Marton 1997, 99). Instead, phenomenographic research aims to explore the phenomenon within the whole sample group, ignoring individuals within the group (Franke & Dahlgren 1996, 630; Åkerlind 2005a, 323). The collective nature of categories is described by Marton and Booth (1997):

> The description we reach is … a description on the collective level, and in that sense individual voices are not heard… the specific flavours, the scents, and the colours of the worlds of the individuals have been abandoned. (Marton & Booth 1997, 114)

Consequently, when analysing his/her data, the phenomenographer looks for consistencies and differences primarily across rather than within the individuals' expressions regarding their experiences (e.g. Marton, Watkins & Tang 1997, 25).

In analysis, the researcher should maintain the phenomenographic principle of a second-order perspective. That implies, according to Hasselgren and Beach (1997, 192), "living the experience of a phenomenon vicariously, by stepping back from one's own experiences and using it only to illuminate the ways in which others state an understanding for something." It is also important to be aware that a phenomenographer is not trying to describe in any objective sense how the human beings experience the phenomenon, but rather how they describe their experiences. Hence, as a result of the analysis, the categories of description and the outcome space actually do not, after all, represent anything but the relationship between the transcripts and the analyst. (Prosser et al. 2005, 140-141.)

In the following sections I will illustrate the practices used when analysing the empirical data of the current research. That illustration, however, concerns solely my primary interview data. The supplementary triangulation data in the form of written accounts followed similar steps of analysis and is therefore not separately handled here.

6.4.1 Preparations for Analysis

After each interview, I immediately checked the quality of the tapes by listening through them. On the whole the recordings were of good quality. However, on a few occasions the interviewee's voice was quite low, and therefore, while I still remembered what had been said in the course of the interview, I directly wrote those parts down. The tape-recorded interviews were transcribed verbatim (see e.g. Marton 1997, 99) by a research assistant into a set of text files. Transcribing means that the verbal data is de-contextualised, the conversational context is de-emphasised, and the context in the text emphasised (Dortins 2002, 209). Kvale (1996, 165) considers a transcription a translation both from spoken to written language, and from living and personal conversation to a frozen text, which is to be read analytically.

The typist had already completed several tasks of the same kind, i.e. she was used to transcribing interviews, also with regard to the field of education. I briefed her to transcribe all that was clearly audible on the tapes, including unfinished sentences, repetitions and vocalised hesitations. In situations of fuzzy recordings (interviewer's and interviewee's turns overlapped, participant's voice too low, and so on) she was instructed not to guess what was said, but instead to draw my attention to those unintelligible parts. I further advised her to ignore laughter and groaning, or pauses, etc. The reason for excluding these from the text was that, after having listened to the tapes several times, I had well caught the emotions in them. I also thought those expressions might be disruptive when concentrating on what was really said. Technical details (font, line) and the layout of the text were also outlined to her. The transcription took place without delay during the summer months of 2002. The total time needed for this was around two months.

Copies of the transcribed interviews were not sent to the participants to refine, correct or complete (face validity check). Within the phenomenographic research approach this is not considered necessary because different situations call for different experiences (i.e. because of the relational nature of phenomenographic data, see Chapter 3, and the dynamic nature of awareness, see Section 4.1.1). In other words, people's experiences are influenced by their intentions and the context in which the phenomena occur (e.g. Boulton-Lewis 2000). From the perspective of the current research, what was said was said in the interview situations (e.g. Krogsmark 2006 in press), and the ideas falling outside that situation were taken as irrelevant in the sense that they represented another situation within participants' experience. After transcription was completed I checked the texts against the tapes and made the refinements needed. At the same time my attention was already directed towards gaining some tentative impressions of what the interviewees were saying with regard to their learning.

The text files were then fed separately into a qualitative data processing software program NVivo 6.1. (see e.g. Fraser 2000; Luomanen & Räsänen 2002) and annotated with relevant identification details. That program was used as a technical tool when analysing the data. According to my experience, NVivo makes it easier to handle qualitative data systematically and in a controlled way, contributing to the rigour of the research. Especially in a phenomenographic research, where the analysis requires a great deal of repetitive manipulation of text, that kind of program is of great use.

6.4.2 *Phases of Analysis*

The process of analysis involved five different phases, which were in accordance, though adapted, with Sandberg's (1994, 86) phases of a phenomenographic analysis (see also Bruce 1997). While the whole process was decidedly iterative (e.g. Åkerlind 2005a, 324), the boundaries between different phases were vaguer than my linear description of them below would suggest. Although each phase plays an essential role in the construction of the categories and outcome space, in practice the stages should be seen as being interactive. As noted by Marton (1997, 100), while each successive stage has implications not only for the phases that go after it but also for the phases that come before it, the analysis has to go through several cycles in which the different phases are considered to some extent simultaneously.

The phases of analysis followed in the present research were

1. becoming familiar with the transcripts
2. discovering the referential dimensions of experiencing learning
3. discovering the structural dimensions of experiencing learning
4. establishing the categories of description
5. establishing the outcome space.

In the analysis I used the framework of the anatomy of awareness (Marton & Booth 1997) (see Section 4.1.1). Within that framework a particular way of experiencing a phenomenon (here learning) can be seen as a mirror image of particular features of human being's awareness and subsequently varying ways of experiencing that phenomenon can be seen as mirror images of diverse awareness. This idea is captured in Figure 4 below. For the research reported here this means that each category of experiencing learning corresponds to particular features of awareness.

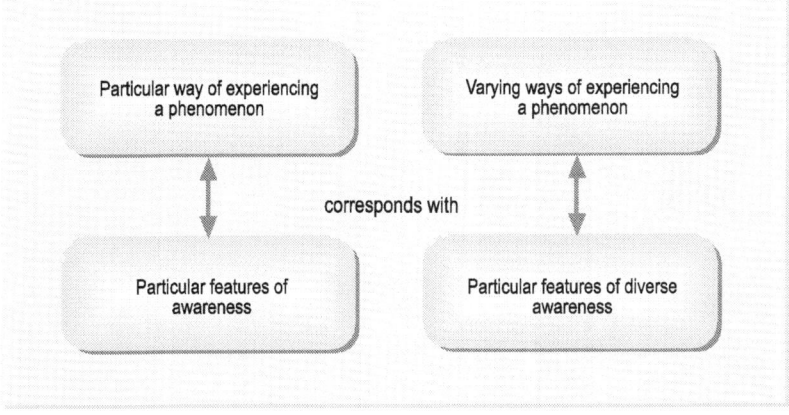

Figure 4. Relationship between way(s) of experiencing and features of awareness

In order to help me focus on the most essential points in the analysis, I defined precise aims and guiding core questions for each phase (see e.g. Bruce 1997; Cope 2002; Kirk 2002). Those analytical tools were also employed to help the reader trace the process by which my results were arrived at (see Ashworth and Lucas 2000, 300). In addition, the analysis adapted principles given by several authors on phenomenography, for example, Bruce 1997; Marton 1997; Marton & Booth 1997; Ashworth and Lucas 2000; Åkerlind 2002b, 2005a.

Becoming familiar with the transcripts

Aim: To identify from the transcripts what has been said about the experience of learning.
Core questions: What does the transcript tell me about the ways the learners experience their learning?

Practices employed:
When starting to analyse, I tried to take into account Wood's (2000, 79; see also Åkerlind 2005a, 324) advice that the researcher should first immerse him-/herself in the data with an open attitude, and then progressively become more focused on certain aspects. Open attitude implies, among other things, that the researcher should be free of preconceived ideas of his/her own (see epoché in Section 6.2.1) considering the phenomenon in question (see Marton 1997, 99; Francis, 1996, 43; Ashworth & Lucas 2000, 300).

I first read the transcripts several times in order to obtain a tentative understanding of what was in general said about the ways of experiencing learning. I noticed that with each rereading a more sophisticated understanding of the learners' ways of experiencing emerged. During the first rounds of reading I concentrated on identifying the broad lines in experiencing, whereas in the subsequent rounds I read the transcripts trying to identify some sort of differences among the ways of experiencing.

Contrary to the customary fashion in qualitative research, I did not define any unit of analyses beforehand, because one's experiences can be expressed in many kinds of different units (e.g. in separate sentences, in the groups of sentences, or in paragraphs). Furthermore, one must bear in mind that experiences may also exist within each other or overlap one another. Therefore, the same text segment can include more than one kind of analytic units (expression of experiences). In addition, as noted by Franke and Dahlgren (1996, 630), expressions often represent different fragments of the same experience (i.e. belong to the same whole).

After an extended period of reading I started to progressively reduce my data by distinguishing and making choices between what was relevant from the point of view of experiencing learning and what was not. Naturally, because of the iterative nature of the analysis, the matter of assigning value was confronted several times throughout the analysis.

Until this point in the analysis, I had carried out the process by working within each individual transcript. That is to say, I handled one transcript at a time by looking for the differences and similarities in expressions with regard to experiences of learning. Similarities and differences relate to the fact that as a researcher, one must decide whether the utterances are different expressions of the same experience or if they refer to different experiences (Franke & Dahlgren 1996, 630). I marked and segmented the distinct expressions in transcripts according to the experiences addressed. The distinct experiences were highlighted with different colours. Marton and Pong (2005, 337) suggest that a unit of experience (expression of experience) can be formed whenever there is sufficient evidence that a particular overall meaning has been expressed.

In this part of the analysis my comparisons of differences and similarities concerning different experiences were still made on a rather superficial level. However, simultaneously with the marking and segmenting procedures I started to write tentative definitions (criterion attributes) for each segment (representing various experiences) in order to remember the essential features behind them during the next round of iteration.

The marked and segmented expressions of experiencing learning taken from the transcripts formed my data pool for the further analysis. What was seen as relevant data in relation to learners' ways of experiencing learning was now among that data. Marton (1997, 100) stipulates that each expression has two contexts in relation to which it has to be interpreted. The first is the transcript from which it was taken and the other the pool of data to which it belongs. That is to say that, in phenomenography, "no one transcript can be understood in isolation from the others. Every transcript, or expression of meaning, is interpreted within the context of the group of transcripts or meanings as a whole, in terms of similarities to and differences from other transcripts or meanings" (Åkerlind 2005a, 323 referring to Åkerlind, Bowden & Green in press). At this stage I therefore turned my attention from the level of individual to a collective level. The boundaries separating learners were now abandoned (but only temporarily) and my interest was instead focused on the data pool. (Åkerlind 2005a, 325.)

The expressions marked were then extracted from transcripts (i.e. decontextualized from their original context) in the form of quotes, and brought together into tentative categories on the basis of the similarities in experiencing learning. It is important to note here that in every transcript, more than one category can be, and often is, represented (Prosser et al. 2005, 141). The extracted quotes contained 512 paragraphs of text, one paragraph denoting one quote. After extraction, each quote could still always be precisely positioned into the transcript at the place it came from (due to my using NVivo program). In addition, each quote was certainly also viewable in isolation or within its new category context.

As a result of the first phase of analysis, I had identified what had been said about the ways of experiencing learning by distinguishing from the transcripts what was relevant from the point of view of the matter in question. The identification let me generate a tentative set of categories concerning varying ways of experiencing learning. In phenomenography an experience usually differs both with regard to a global meaning of a certain phenomenon (the referential dimension) and with regard to how a certain phenomenon and its component parts are delimited and related to each other (the structural dimension) (Beaty, Dall'Alba & Marton 1990, 2). Therefore, my analysis continued by discovering first the referential dimensions of experiencing learning and then the structural dimensions.

Discovering the referential dimension

Aim: To identify the overall meanings (or variations in meanings) of the different ways of experiencing learning.
Core questions: In what qualitatively different ways are the learners experiencing their learning here? How might the statement: "Learning is experienced as ..." be completed on the basis of my data? (Bruce 1997, 105).

Practices employed:
"Referential aspect is a particular meaning of an individual object" (here object of learning) experienced; it is "anything delimited and attended to by subjects" (Marton & Pong 2005, 336). Accordingly, from this point onwards my task was to delve deeper into the meanings (variations in meanings) beyond those 512 separate expressions (quotes) within the developing set of categorisation system generated in the previous phase of analysis.

In practice, discovering the referential dimension followed an iterative process similar to the first phase of the analysis, but with some important differences. While the first phase concentrated mainly on finding variations within individual learners' transcripts, this phase concentrated on defining meanings beyond those variations within the whole data. Therefore I continued the analysis on the basis of similarities, differences and complementarities across the entire data, by comparing each quote with all the other quotes until clear and coherent meanings beyond them had been established. The separate quotes were in constant movement, changing their place from one category to another according to the meaning they addressed. As a consequence of this iteration new tentative categories emerged, old ones disappeared and some merged. The criterion attributes for each category were then refined in an attempt to describe the most essential meanings of each category (i.e. ways of experiencing learning).

When the various expressions are compared with each other, it is crucial to recognise that it is the various meanings underlying the expressions and not the linguistic expressions themselves that are to be compared. What counts as same experiences may be expressed in many linguistically different ways, and vice versa, what counts as different experiences may likewise be expressed in similar language. (Svensson 1994, 19.) Marton (1997, 100) presents two heuristic tools which were also applied here, and through which a certain experiencing appears. According to him, when it is discovered that two expressions which are different at the word level reflect the same meaning, we may become aware of a certain way of experiencing the phenomenon. Whereas when two expressions reflect two different meanings, two ways of experiencing the phenomenon may become thematised due to that contrast effect. Hence, the researcher has to study the data first and foremost with the intention of understanding what the learners are expressing, irrespective which words they use (Dahlgren 1997, 29). It is therefore possible that there are wide linguistic variations among expressions belonging to the same category. On occasions where the meaning underlying an expression was vague or illogical I viewed that expression in its original transcript context. I took into consideration what was said before and after that expression and evaluated the meaning in the light of those connections. This is parallel to a hermeneutic cycle which explicates the meaning of a text through an increasing understanding of the whole from the parts of the text, the parts from the whole, and so on (see Kvale 1996).

As a result of the second phase of the analysis I had captured the overall meanings of the various ways of experiencing learning. However, due to the consecutive nature of the analysis they were still subject to alterations. Now I was also able to tentatively complete the statement "Learning is experienced as...". In the next phase, the exploring of meaning is supplemented by a search for structural relationships between those meanings.

Discovering the structural dimension

Aim: To identify the structural dimensions of different ways of experiencing learning.
Core questions: What did the learners focus on when experiencing learning in this way? What was focal (in the theme) and what remained the background (in the thematic field) for the learners in their different ways of experiencing learning?

Practices employed:

The structural dimension of experiencing a phenomenon is defined by Marton and Pong (2005, 336) as "the combination of features discerned and focused upon by the subject." The third stage of the analysis often takes place in parallel with the previous, referential, phase. Referring to that simultaneity Marton and Booth (1997, 87) suggest that "structure presupposes meaning and at the same time meaning presupposes structure" and that both occur simultaneously when an individual experiences a phenomenon. At this phase of the analysis I focused on finding the structural dimensions of each way of experiencing learning. In practice I followed the process illustrated by Marton and Pong (2005) (the italics are made by the authors)

> The experiences, now denoted by the various overall meanings, were studied in detail, to identify within each unit the elements of the phenomenon that were focused upon, and to devise a description of each conception's *structural aspect*. In doing so, we paid attention to the explicit *variations* that the student brought in as they focused on a particular element, as well as the *variations* that were implied by that element. (Marton & Pong 2005, 337)

As becomes amply apparent from the citation above, this phase of analysis is more than just a data sorting activity. It requires the researcher to again explore every way of experiencing from the point of view of "the explicit variations that the students brought in as they focused on" their learning. From the perspective of the present research, the ways of experiencing learning underlying each category (as well as each expression in the same category) were now considered in terms of awareness. With the help of the guiding questions and a heuristic tool of a structure of awareness I then sought to discover what was figural to the learners with regard to the different ways of experiencing. For that purpose I made several cross-charts to make clearer to myself what the learners had focused on when experiencing learning in a certain way. This part of the analysis was done manually. The dimensions I particularly looked into and compared with each other with the help of cross-charts were

- focus of intention
- nature of knowledge: ranging from dualistic to relational
- type of knowledge: ranging from quantitative and atomistic to qualitative and holistic
- focus of attention: ranging from sign to significant
- locus of learning: ranging from external to internal

After having finally discovered the structural dimensions of the ways of experiencing learning I classified the experiences with structure and meaning in common to as belonging to the same category of description (see Prosser et al. 2005, 141). At this point of analysis it seemed to me that the iterative process of analysis was reasonable, particularly for the phases of discovering the meaning and structural dimensions of the experiences.

Establishing the categories of description

Aim: To identify the different ways of experiencing learning and describe them in a hierarchical manner.
Questions: What are the different ways of experiencing learning and what is their relation to each other?

Practices employed:
As was mentioned at the beginning of this chapter, the aim of the analysis is to yield descriptive categories of qualitative variation in data. Usually, and as was also the case here, the researcher starts with a comparatively large number of categories, which he/she then gradually, through consecutive iterative stages, defines, arriving at a smaller set of categories that can be reduced no further (e.g. Dahlgren 1997, 29). When starting this fourth phase of analysis, I had in total twentyone tentative categories which were now subjected to the final iteration, that is, they were progressively revised.

Thus, since during the fourth phase the different categories themselves are compared and contrasted, I shifted my attention more markedly from the relationships between separate ways of experiencing to the relationships between the different (21) categories. My aim was now to refine the essential features of each category and give myself a clear understanding of the fundamental variations between the categories. I went on analysing by comparing and contrasting one category at a time with the other categories; what was similar within the category and what was different between the categories. Simultaneously with that activity I sought to formulate progressively more complete and refined descriptions of each category (see Åkerlind 2005a, 325).

The ordering of categories and the positioning of hierarchical relationships between them was constituted through interactive alternation between searching for logical and empirical evidence of inclusiveness and completeness (see e.g. Åkerlind 2002b). By working this way for some time I was able to develop a set of categories which characterised the variation in the ways how learning was experienced by the learners on the basis of my data. These categories were logically interrelated and to a great extent hierarchical.

In arriving at a smaller set of categories the rule of parsimony (see Marton & Booth 1997, 125-126) was taken into account. This means that the researcher should conclude the process with a minimum number of categories which explain all the variations in the data. As a result of this phase I had constructed four main categories, two of which had four subcategories and the other two none. This set of descriptive categories is shown in Chapter 7, Figure 5.

Establishing the outcome space

Aim: To constitute a diagrammatic representation of the logical relationships between the different ways of experiencing learning.
Core questions: What is the logical relation among the categories describing the experiencing of learning?

Practices employed:
Marton (1997, 100) refers to an outcome space as an ordered complex of categories of descriptions. More precisely, according to Bruce (1997, 87), it is a diagrammatic representation of the logical relationships between the different experiences of a phenomenon. It does not constitute phenomena in the surrounding world, but rather people's various ways of thinking about their experiences (Sjöström & Dahlgren 2002, 342). Outcome space elucidates relationships between and within the different descriptive categories of the same whole,

allowing more profound meaning to be derived from the analysis. The highlighting of logical relationships provides a way of looking at a phenomenon holistically (Åkerlind 2005b, 8). Although each category may be presented as consisting of a combination of different aspects, this is for descriptive and analytic purposes. The experience represented by each category of description would be a holistic one, and necessarily different from the sum of its parts or aspects. (Åkerlind 2005b, 21.)

According to Åkerlind (2005a, 323), a perfect outcome space symbolizes a full range of possible ways of experiencing the phenomenon in question at a particular point in time for the population represented by the sample group. The outcome space of the present research is presented in Chapter 7, Figure 6. When that outcome space was designed there was no more iteration of data. Instead, that activity was on the one hand based on the referential and structural dimensions of categories and on the other hand on the researcher's developing theoretical understanding of the phenomenon in question.

This section described the different phases of the analysis of my empirical data concerning TUKEVA students' ways of experiencing their learning. All the phases were revisited several times in the course of the analysis to confirm and adjust the interpretations made in the process towards constructing the descriptive categories and the outcome space. The results of the research are presented in the next chapter (Chapter 7).

7 RESULTS: ADULT LEARNERS' WAYS OF EXPERIENCING LEARNING AND PHENOMENOGRAPHY AS A RESEARCH APPROACH

This chapter presents the results of a phenomenographic study on adult learners' learning as university students. The task of the research was to explore the ways the adult learners experienced their learning and described the variation in it. The results of a phenomenographic study consist of diverse ways of experiencing the phenomenon under investigation. According to the theory of learning and awareness (Marton & Booth 1997; Bowden & Marton 2004; Marton et al. 2004) used as a framework for the present research, a particular way of experiencing a phenomenon corresponds to a particular pattern of aspects of the phenomenon in the learner's focal awareness, i.e. the theme of awareness.

As is customary in phenomenographic research, the results are presented here as a set of descriptive categories in an outcome space, symbolizing a range of qualitatively different ways of experiencing the phenomenon as well as features of diverse awareness. The outcome space forms an inclusive, hierarchical unity in which the categories further up in the hierarchy subsume those preceding them. (e.g. Åkerlind 2005a, 2005b.)

The categories in this research are representations of learners' experiences of learning identified by the researcher in the course of the interpretative analysis of the data. It is, however, important to note that the categories are not meant to be identical with one individual learner's experiences but are seen as exemplifying features of the whole phenomena of learning drawn by all the participants of the research.

Following the recommendations of Åkerlind (2005a, 10-11), the results are accounted in two interrelated ways: through
- descriptions of key aspects of the variation in experience representing the range of qualitatively different ways of experiencing learning
- common themes of variation running through the categories. These themes mark the structure of the outcome space by delineating logical relationships between the categories.

7.1 Categories of Description

In response to the first research question: What kind of variation is there in adult learners' ways of experiencing their learning at a university, four qualitatively distinct main categories of description were composed. The categories were differentiated from each other by variation along four dimensions: cognition, practice, self-regulation, and professional growth and development. Learning was correspondingly experienced as:

A. Cognitive Phases of Learning
B. Integration of Theory and Practice
C. Self-Regulation of Learning
D. Professional Growth and Development.

The categories with their subcategories are presented as a preliminary outcome space in Figure 5.

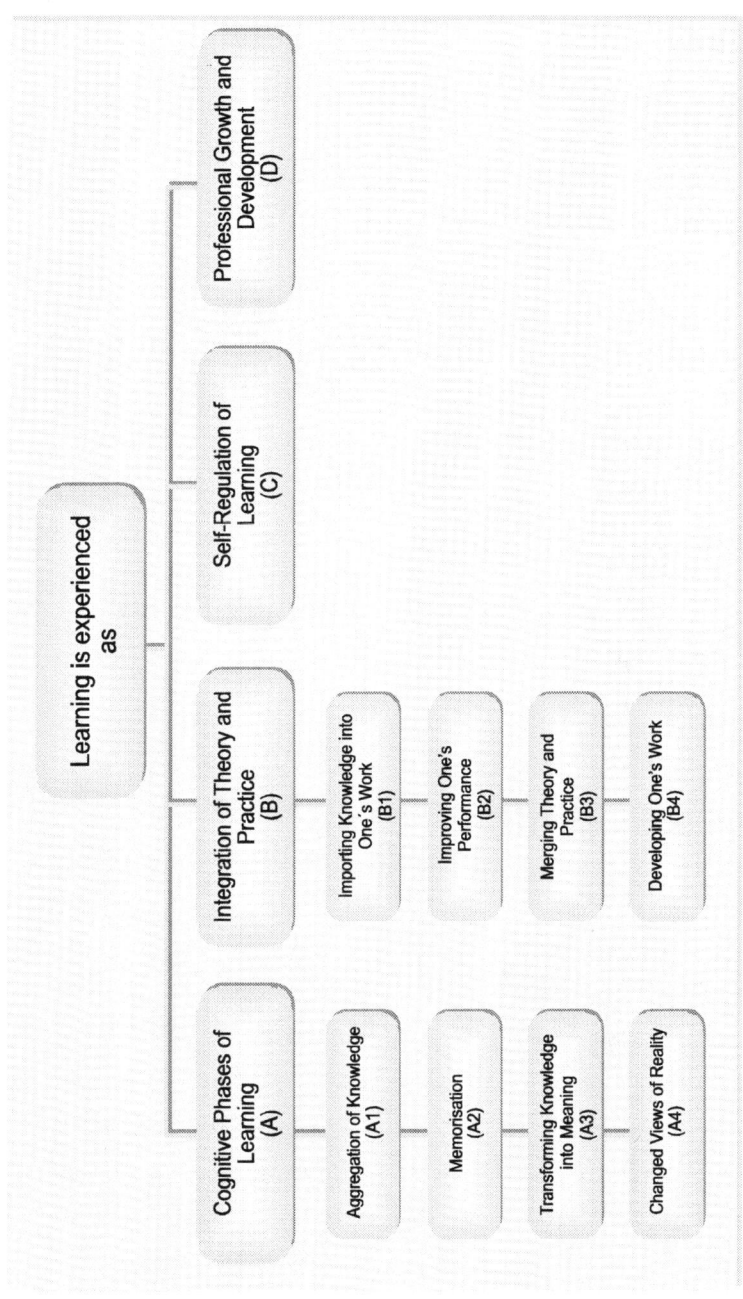

Figure 5. Preliminary outcome space of the ways of experiencing learning

In keeping with phenomenographic research each of the above categories is connected with different meanings given to the experience of learning by the learners. Due to the diversity in experiences, the categories are also associated with different awareness structures of learners. (e.g. Marton & Booth 1997). The categories have been named according to their key features. These are features that the learners have discerned and at the same time kept in their focal awareness (i.e. theme of awareness).

As the categories represent relationships between theory and empirical data (e.g. Svensson & Theman 1983, 20), empirical evidence of preferred categories should be provided by the researcher. Hence the results here are presented so that the theoretical principles are connected to empirical examples in order to bring out the findings of the research. The empirical evidence is provided in the form of relevant quotes from the data. While the quotes give evidence of the researcher's interpretations, they also enrich the description with the voices of the participants. In addition, I hope that they give the reader a sense of authenticity with regard to the experiences of the learners.

The quotes are translated from Finnish into English. Before translation the irrelevant repetitions, digressions as well as interjections have been removed. In order to complete partial sentences there are, when necessary, words in brackets, added by myself. Three successive dots indicate that several words or a sentence or sentences have been removed as irrelevant in relation to the meaning that the quote is intended to illustrate. Neither is there any kind of codes or names of participants in connection with the quotes. These are ignored, on the one hand, for ethical reasons and, on the other hand, because phenomenographers' interest is not in individuals but in collectives. However, to locate the source of evidence I used numbers of interviews and paragraphs. Different interview numbers indicate different interviews.

Moreover, it needs to be pointed out that in phenomenographic research in general, the participants typically identify with more than just one category. This is also the case in the present research. There are categories with which several learners identify, as well as categories with which only few of them identify.

In the following sections the preferred set of categories will be described and elucidated more fully, **giving a comprehensive answer to the first research question: What kind of variation is there in adult learners' ways of experiencing their learning at a university?** This description leads progressively to a response to the second research question: **What kind of a holistic view can be constituted from adult learners' various ways of experiencing their learning at a university?** The answer to the second research question is finally given in the form of an **outcome space** in Figure 6.

The categories are demonstrated below in the same order (A, B, C, D) as they were presented above.

7.2 Cognitive Phases of Learning

This main category, learning as Cognitive Phases of Learning, focuses on what is happening within the minds of the learners. According to this view, learners' ways of experiencing learning seem to be a matter of pure cognition. The category is divided into four qualitatively distinct sub-categories according to the critical aspects focused on by the learners. The sub-categories are learning as (the arrow indicates movement from simple to more complete ways of experiencing learning):

A1. Aggregation of Knowledge
A2. Memorisation
A3. Transforming Knowledge into Meaning
A4. Changed Views of Reality

These four different sub-categories, which represent distinct ways of experiencing learning, are seen here as hierarchically linked. Hierarchy is based on their inclusiveness and relative completeness. Therefore, the experiences in later categories include elements similar to the earlier ones, but not vice versa. (see e.g. Åkerlind 2005a, 11.) Hence, the sub-categories here can be seen as constituting a gradual expansion of learners' cognitive awareness. It is also important to note that while each more complete category has elements in common with all the less complete categories, they should also bring something new and unique in the experience of learning (e.g. Åkerlind 2005a, 11).

Furthermore, according to phenomenographical principles, as discussed previously, an experience has a referential aspect and a structural aspect. Referential aspect denotes the particular meaning learning has for adult learners and structural aspect the combination of features focused upon by the learners. These two aspects, though presented separately, are interrelated. The referential and structural aspects of the experience of learning as Cognitive Phases of Learning are presented in Table 7.

Table 7. *Referential and structural aspects of the experience of learning as Cognitive Phases of Learning*

	CATEGORY A: Learning as Cognitive Phases of Learning	
Experience	Referential aspect	Structural aspect
A1	Learning as aggregation of knowledge	Focus on adding quantifiable knowledge
A2	Learning as memorisation	Focus on holding knowledge in mind
A3	Learning as transforming knowledge into meaning	Focus on making meaning out of phenomena
A4	Learning as changed views of reality	Focus on conceptual change

In the following sections the four sub-categories with regard to the learning as Cognitive Phases of Learning category are described in detail.

7.2.1 Aggregation of Knowledge

> You get information, there's so much of it. (Interview 4, Paragraph 68)

In the category of Aggregation of Knowledge, (A1), the learners are aware of their learning in terms of adding new, quantifiable knowledge to their existing knowledge. The simultaneous discernment of elements such as taking bits of knowledge in, adding to one's knowledge and gaining new knowledge characterised all those expressions describing this experience. As clearly shown in the following quote, acquiring more knowledge about things seems to be the main purpose of learning.

> I'm sure I've learned a lot. One good thing about learning is that the more information you learn the better you realize how little you know. On the other hand... I've noticed that I also have a lot of knowledge. (Interview 10, Paragraph 82)

The point of learning, its value and justification, rests on knowing a lot of things without any terminal point. The idea of learning seems to be that the more things you know the better your learning is. This idea becomes apparent from the quotes below.

> You appreciate the amount of knowledge. It increases all the time. (Interview 16, Paragraph 168)
>
> When you somehow think that you know something about things, so it has been satisfying to notice [how your knowledge increases]. (Interview 6, Paragraph 90)

In all four quotes above, the emphasis is clearly on a quantifiable view of learning. Burnett, Pillay and Dart (2003, 56) note that such a view is considered with acquisition and accumulation of content while missing the point of substance. The present data supported this view. The knowledge acquired by the learners was associated with isolated parts of substance, instead of integrated ones. Presumably for that reason the learners felt themselves incapable of organising their knowledge into more sophisticated form, as shown in the quote below.

> ... some kind of general knowledge... quite useful... it can't really be broken down. (Interview 8, Paragraph 104)

The learners also saw no possibilities for applying their knowledge. They felt that they had accumulated new knowledge, but they did not know how to make use of it. This kind of situation was put into words by one participant: "You know so many things but real life is something very different". This worthlessness of knowledge also becomes apparent in the two quotes below.

> ...all kinds of things, mostly general knowledge. They're quite interesting subjects. I just don't know where I could make good use of them, at least at the moment. (Interview 8, Paragraph 104)
>
> I guess I've read a lot of theoretical information from books. The thing is who knows how to apply it. (Interview 4, Paragraph 64)

The learners seem to focus on what Biggs (2003, 15 referring to Marton) calls signs learning. The term refers to picking up isolated parts of content and treating those parts independently of each other. Like Burnett et al. (2003), Biggs (2003, 15) also suggests that the learning of signs prevents learners from seeing what the signs signify, i.e. they do not grasp either the meaning or structure of what is meant to be learnt. When illuminating this kind of learning, Biggs (ibid.) uses an apt metaphor: "The learners cannot see the wood for the trees."

The experiences of learning in this category also seem to support the view of some kind of ready-made knowledge. As the two quotes below clearly show, the learners felt that there are places (e.g. books as demonstrated by the previous quote) where knowledge is stored and where one can look for knowledge, check up on one's knowledge and effortlessly collect more knowledge when needed.

> I mean it has given you a kind of refuge. So that there are places where you can check the information, you get information easily. (Interview 6, Paragraph 90)
>
> ...another thing is that I've learned well to read and look for information. (Interview 13, Paragraph 146)

In this sub-category the learners did not seem to be agents of their learning. It rather seems that learning (knowledge) takes place as a result of a delivery of knowledge made by someone outside the learner. This became evident, for instance, in the way the learners spoke about their learning, i.e. what kind of words they used when expressing themselves. As they, for instance, repeatedly used such term as "learning comes", it gave the impression that the learners did not consider themselves as agents of their learning but, instead, looked for someone else to equip them with the relevant knowledge.

7.2.2 Memorisation

> I have to memorise the information right away or I lose it. (Interview 13, Paragraph 146)

In the category of Memorisation, (A2), the learners are aware of their learning in terms of retaining knowledge in their minds, that is, being able to memorise (remember) things from the material to be learned. On a general level, memorising is not considered (e.g. Dahlin & Regmi

1997, 477) to be a good way of learning. Dahlin and Regmi (ibid., 477-478) suggest that memorisation may be helpful in preparation for some test situations but worthless in the sense of understanding the subject matter. The intention in memorising is (ibid.) to let the knowledge from the learning source enter into the learner's memory and be stored in the brain.

In relation to the present sub-category, learning as Memorisation, there are two overlapping terms in the literature, rote learning and memorising. Dahlin and Regmi (1997, 477) have noted that particularly in the Western learning context, memorising something and learning it in parrot-fashion (i.e. rote learning) often have quite equal meanings. The observations of Asian learners, on the other hand, seem to indicate (Marton and Booth 1997, 44) that memorising can as well be associated with understanding. However, rote learning is considered (e.g. Dahlin & Regmi 1997, 482) to lead to short-term learning and is applicable only in assessment situations, whereas the effects of memorisation are thought to be more long-lasting and also to reach beyond the educational context.

Some of the learners' statements here (for example the quote below) greatly resembled a kind of rote learning. Dahlin and Regmi (1997, 478) argue that the rote learning strategy is used particularly in situations where the learner suffers from lack of understanding. It is also used on occasions where the learner is not interested enough to pay attention to the subject matter. A negative point considering rote learning is, as noted by Dahlin and Regmi (ibid), that it does not involve any assimilation of knowledge but just words that can be repeated when needed. The quote below exemplifies the idea of rote learning very well, likewise the key features of this sub-category:

> I've learned that I have to memorise things at once to remember them later. (Interview 13, Paragraph 146)

Entwistle and Entwistle (2003, 36) characterise memorising as "a largely mechanical, unreflective process of forcing knowledge into memory by conscious effort". The next quote (as well as the previous one) gives evidence of a conscious attempt to force knowledge into one's head.

> I've decided that when I read I do it so that I remember them. Not just look at them. (Interview 13, Paragraph 146)

Dahlin and Regmi (1997, 482) see that repetition of knowledge is a part of memorisation. Repetition constitutes a link between rote learning and memorisation. In this research the learners felt that the repetition of old things, once learnt and then forgotten, brought them back into memory. Beairsto (1996, 94) also argues that in some cases memorising can be simply a matter of bringing forgotten concepts back into the foreground of awareness. With regard to the same topic Jarvis (2004, 71) suggests that in familiar situations the knowledge gained may merely reinforce that which the individual already has, as seems to be the case below.

> …and it was then again repeating old things… Sometimes in working life I had done those tasks. Sometimes while studying I had got to know them. And that way the things came back to me… that had sometimes been a part of my life in work. (Interview 7, Paragraph 126)

The ability to memorise and recall are the focus of the discussion concerning the next two quotes. Recalling is usually (see e.g. Dahlin & Regmi 1997, 478), both in the present research and the examples below, associated with situations of reproduction in a form of assessment. As stated by Dahlin and Regmi (ibid.), in recalling a mechanical memory of sequences of words is established for assessment purposes, but is forgotten after it has fulfilled this function (sometimes even before that).

> …I have thought about some parts that they are just things that I had to do. (Interview 3, Paragraph 30)

> …studying has mostly been doing exams. Because there are only a little contact classes my emphasis is on getting through exams. I sometimes feel that even though I pass the exams I'm not sure whether I know any more than before the exam. (Interview 8, Paragraph 26)

In the next quotes the learners' focus is on gaining a qualification with pass-only aspiration, i.e. just getting through the studies in order to have the academic degree. With a pass-only ambition, learning becomes emotionally a drag, a task to be got out of the way, (Biggs 2003, 15), as is demonstrated by the first quote below. If the learners consider their learning as merely a quantifiable increase of knowledge, or a memorisation task they will, according to Trigwell & Prosser (1997, 243), have difficulties in adopting such learning strategies that lead to high quality learning. In the second quote below, Trigwell and Prosser's message becomes visible in the form of the learner's poor self-confidence concerning the quality of his/her learning when adopting a pass-only aspiration strategy.

> My first goal is to get the degree, so that the time I spend wouldn't be just for fun. (Interview 8, Paragraph 26)

> Gathering studies has been mostly doing one exam after the other. I guess you get a feeling that do I really know about these things? ...I have completed the university-level degree, which was the highest you can do in this country. And still I felt that the knowledge was quite superficial...Of course you could read the books very deeply but time is limited. You just do what you think is needed to get through the exam. (Interview 14, Paragraph 102)

The next quote combines the main features of the former (A1 Aggregation of Knowledge) and the present (A2 Memorisation) category. In the course of learning the learners have accumulated a lot of knowledge (memory) and as a result they know numerous facts about the subjects to be learnt. However, despite the huge amount of knowledge the learners feel they have, they see themselves as unable to use that knowledge in real life, because "real-life is something else" as one learner expressed it. Finding no connections between knowledge and its use, the learners did not manage to retain the information that they had accumulated in their memories. The quote below illustrates the temporary nature of this kind of learning discussed in categories A1 and A2: gaining knowledge, making (or trying to make) use of it, memorising it or losing it.

> Take, for example, education or leadership, you know quite a bit about them, but real life is different after all. You can't always remember the things you've learned even though they are good in a way. (Interview 7, Paragraph 130)

7.2.3 Transforming Knowledge into Meaning

> The paths of thinking, between the ears, are becoming stronger. (Interview 15, Paragraph 90)

The experience of learning in the category of Transforming Knowledge into Meaning, (A3), comes close to what Bowden (2004) has termed knowledge capability. That is an

> ...ability to handle previously unseen, real-life situations, to make sense of them, to figure out what the relevant aspects are, to relate them to what you know and to find out what you don't know but need to use (Bowden 2004, 40)

In this category the learners are aware of their learning in terms of making meaning out of phenomena. Bowden and Marton (2004, 36) define the meaning of a phenomenon as "a function of what it is related to". For Mezirow (1996), making meaning involves learning with established frames of reference and learning to transform them. He claims that we do not make meaning by attaching a predefined meaning to a word but by transforming our old frames of reference. By so doing, we do not just learn new understandings, but we also learn new ways to understand something (ibid, 3).

When considering the value of knowledge Pring (2005, 90) proposes that as "…bodies of knowledge do not have value independently of people finding value in them, so too propositions, theories, arguments do not have meaning unless people find them meaningful – unless they connect with the learners' way of making sense of experience." Pring's (ibid.) line of reasoning means that in order to transform information into meaning the learner must make sense of the information encountered. Limberg (1999) has the same idea when he proposes that in order to be more knowledgeable in subject matter implies a qualitative change to a deeper and more complex understanding of a phenomenon.

The terms 'meaning' and 'understanding', mentioned above, form the core of this way of experiencing learning, corresponding to particular features in learners' awareness. Due to their centrality in the present sub-category, the terms are discussed further below.

Haggis (2003, 94) sees meaning as a very wide-ranging and non-specific issue that can be interpreted in a variety of ways. One way to interpret it is to find connections of the phenomenon within its subject area (i.e. "function of what it is related to"). Meaning, in that sense, is defined from outside the learner, usually by a discipline or by a teacher. This kind of meaning is not easily accessible to learners who are acting outside that subject area, as many of the participants of the present research were. The other kind of meaning is personal meaning given to phenomena by the learners themselves. In a university context this personal meaning is controlled by disciplinary boundaries, cultural norms and assessment mechanisms. (ibid.)

Haggis (2003, 94) continues that there is a similar conceptual difficulty with the term 'understanding' as with 'meaning'. Understanding, like meaning, is non-specific and relative in nature, and therefore inherently problematic. What it signifies in a university context varies according to discipline and teacher, etc. Evaluation of understanding is likely to see it as an achievable and a demonstrable state. However, what counts as understanding, is not at all times a demonstrable state, but, in Haggis (2003, 94) words, a "more complicated idea that is connected with being able to show awareness of conflicting perspectives, an ability to build an argument out of uncertainty, and, above all, to engage in a particular kind of questioning of fundamental values and assumptions."

When considering how the understanding of phenomena comes about Nickerson (1985) points out exactly the same elements as the learners in this research did.

> Understanding is an active process. It requires the connecting of facts, the relating of newly acquired information to what is already known, the weaving of bit of knowledge into an integrated and cohesive whole. In short, it requires not only having knowledge but also doing something with it. (Nickerson 1985, 234)

The learners felt that the prerequisite for understanding is that one does not learn things by rote, as expressed in the quote below. In their research Entwistle and Entwistle (1991) found that the nature of understanding is associated with a feeling of satisfaction. The same mood is mentioned below.

> It's quite a nice feeling to realize that... you can still absorb things and if you don't memorise them by heart at least you understand also such things that you haven't even ever studied before. (Interview 14, Paragraph 114)

How understanding arises was explained by the learners as some kind of sudden illumination or a spark of understanding (quote below). It indicates a move from received knowledge towards more self-constructed ways of knowing. This may be a sign of a mental leap, which has taken place in learners' ways of experiencing their learning.

> Oh, I've learned very much. I even get insights from many things. (Interview 13, Paragraph 146)

The learners also spoke about finally finding something familiar and the right words when reading, for example, newspapers. This tells of the integration of new things with their existing knowledge and might be interpreted as evidence of understanding.

> ...you can finally find something familiar from papers...right words...If nothing else, it maybe helps you in coffee table conversations. (Interview 6, Paragraph 94)

The next two quotes (as well as the previous one) show that making sense of experience includes perceiving connections between different phenomena. Marton and Booth (2004, 7) have demonstrated this kind of process: "Once we have seen a pattern in an ambiguous picture it may be difficult to unsee it" (ibid.). The same is expressed by the learners in the quotes below.

> The things you do in working life that are important there...you're able to connect them...(Interview 6, Paragraph 94)

> And you notice when you talk...with people that you understand more. In a concrete way more of things that people talk about and see the contexts in a different way. (Interview 16, Paragraph 156)

In Dahlin's (1999, 196) research, on ways of coming to understand, understanding was often characterised by the learners as having a grasp of the whole and seeing how things are connected or related, i.e. how they belong together in that whole. The same definition of understanding was stressed by the learners in this research, as is shown by next two quotes below. The learners directed their learning towards making a whole of the parts. Emphasis was placed on ways of perceiving things from different angles. Things were related to other things, or parts of a whole. In addition to that, it appears (first quote below) that the learner is an active agent of his/her learning.

> Perhaps the best thing I've learned is the fact that my own view has become involved. My own view has somehow expanded and control of things has increased... Perhaps it's the bigger entity, the shaping of that has become better. (Interview 10, Paragraph 82)

> I can't necessarily even list theories, I've seen and heard a lot of them but... perhaps regarding learning I have begun to see more entities than details. That means my habit was to try to learn the main points but now I begin to...see these things...first of all they're not black and white and then the fact that they are a kind of entities. (Interview 17, Paragraph 75)

As previously discussed, Haggis (2003, 94) sees understanding as involving an ability to "show awareness of conflicting perspectives...engage in a particular kind of questioning of fundamental values and assumptions" (ibid.). What is said by Haggis (ibid.) is comprehended and handled here as critical thinking or critical being. Mezirow (1996, 1) also links criticality with the process of making meaning. He writes that "we transform our frames of reference by becoming critically reflected of assumptions" and as a consequence of that "we learn new understanding" and "we also learn new ways to understand" (ibid.). The learners reported being more critical towards all kinds of things than earlier, as shown in the quote below.

> One thing… I've learned here is being critical…and I've noticed that there can be so many opinions about the same thing. And any of them isn't right or wrong. They're just opinions… I've been much more black and white before. I've thought some thing is a fact and that's it. Now there are the grey areas there. (Interview 12, Paragraph 102)

The next quote illustrates how learners become critically aware of their assumptions and those of others as well as of assessing their relevance (e.g. Mezirow 2000, 4). As becomes apparent from this quote, critical thinking plays an important role in generating learners' qualified judgements as a result of pooling, considering and structuring the relevant aspects of the situation (e.g. Phillips & Bond 2004, 288). In both quotes (the previous and the next one) of the learners express clearly how they have become critically aware.

> …I notice that I've become more critical… towards many kinds of things. I don't really put up with general remarks. I've noticed that I start to ask questions like… what do you mean and what way, and who said so and when and to whom. (Interview 15, Paragraph 110)

7.2.4 Changed Views of Reality

> I don't seem to fit into the old frameworks any more. (Interview 15, Paragraph 122)

In this category, Changed Views of Reality (A4), the learners are aware of their learning in terms of changed views of reality. When expressing their changed views, the learners used, among others, the following kinds of expressions: "this change in my way of thinking, you see things differently, the self-control and will and ability to see things from many perspectives, I don't seem to fit into the old framework, it's reflected in all I do or think." The meaning of this category lies in the learners' changed thinking about phenomena as a result of learning, and hence viewing the world differently and holding changed views of reality. This kind of change is, in this research, seen as an equivalent of conceptual change.

Considerations of space in this book and its goal do not allow a comprehensive review of conceptual change. However, a short overview of the relevant literature is necessary to describe this category. Conceptual change can be viewed as an outcome or a process. According to Luque (2003, 135 referring to Chi 1992) "outcomes of conceptual change are changes in an individual's knowledge that result as a consequence of the change processes." On the other hand, conceptual change processes, for instance intentional conceptual change, are "the mechanisms by which individuals achieve change in their prior knowledge" (Luque 2003, 135). Enrichment, revision, change in the framework theory (Vosniadou 1994), or radical restructuring of prior knowledge (Chi, Slotta & Leeuw 1994) are examples of the outcomes of conceptual change.

Conceptual change as enrichment implies the accumulation of new information to individuals' old knowledge (Luque 2003, 137 referring to Vosniadou 1994) and resembles here the categories of learning as Aggregation of Knowledge (A1) and Memorisation (A2). However, conceptual change cannot be achieved through those additive mechanisms alone (Vosniadou & Verschaffel 2004, 445). Revision is required when the information to be acquired by the learner is not consistent with his/her beliefs, presuppositions or theories (ibid.). This type of conceptual change has elements in common with the category of learning as Transforming Knowledge into Meaning (A3). Whereas the present category, Changed Views of Reality (A4), resembles Vosniadou's (1994) third type of conceptual change. This involves a revision of the old framework theory. The framework theory represents "relatively coherent systems of explanation, based on everyday experience and tied to years of confirmation" (Vosniadou 1994, 49). With regard to conceptual change one learner actually stated (quote below) that there is no longer room for his/her old framework.

> I feel these studies have opened new views and I have realized that I don't fit anymore to the old frameworks. Things were perhaps easier and more straightforward before the studies began. (Interview 15, Paragraph 122)

For Chi et al. (1994) radical conceptual change means a cognitive shift across different ontological categories, which are matter, process or mental states. Conceptual change occurs when a concept is reassigned from one ontological category to another. The quote below represents an expression that might be interpreted as a radical conceptual change in the learner's mental states. This kind of change is reflected in all the learner does or thinks.

> Our supervisor said that you're now entering a road with no return. You won't ever think about things the way you think now. And I totally subscribe to that. It's reflected to everything you do and think, you have so different ways to think. (Interview 15, Paragraph 110)

When it comes to the process of conceptual change, intentional conceptual change calls attention to the relationship between cognitive, metacognitive, motivational, and emotional factors (Luque 2003, 135). According to Luque (2003, 140-164), such prerequisites as metacognitive, volitional and self-regulation in particular are needed for successful intentional conceptual change to occur. The next quote implies previous kinds of intentional elements concerning the learner's self-control (self-regulation prerequisite), will (volitional prerequisite) and ability (metacognitive prerequisite).

> I have... changed... you're somehow happy from what you've learned but you don't tell everyone about it. That's left behind and now [there's] this composure and the will and ability to look at things from many perspectives. (Interview 5, Paragraph 118)

When considering conceptual change, it is, however, important to note that not all conceptual change implies intentionality (Ruohotie 2005a, 6). However, in the examples that were presented in this category, intentionality seemed to be present.

Table 8 summarises the critical aspect of the range of variation in ways of experiencing learning as Cognitive Phases of Learning.

Table 8. *The range of variation in ways of experiencing learning as Cognitive Phases of Learning*

Themes of expanding awareness	Category			
↱	Aggregation of Knowledge (A1)	Memorisation (A2)	Transforming Knowledge into Meaning (A3)	Changed Views of Reality (A4)
Focus of intention	Adding	Storing and consuming	Making meaning	Conceptual change
Nature of knowledge	Dualistic	Dualistic	Relational	Relational
Type of knowledge	Quantitative	Quantitative	Qualitative	Qualitative
Focus of attention	Sign	Sign	Significant	Significant
Locus of learning	External	External/internal	Internal	Internal

7.3 Integration of Theory and Practice

In this second main category, learning as Integration of Theory and Practice (B), the learners are aware of their learning in terms of combining theory with practice. The key idea behind this category lies in the learners' ways of seeing their learning through the eyes of professionals. The category is related to the concern of declarative and procedural knowledge. As Leinhardt, McCarthy Young, and Merriman (1995, 403) suggest, knowledge acquired in practice is typically procedural in nature, whereas knowledge gained at a university tends to be declarative, i.e. abstract and conceptual. When it comes to adult learners in general, involving participants of the present research, the first kind of knowledge is usually emphasised at the expense of the second. Leinhardt et al. point out that the use of knowledge is context dependent. Practical contexts that are familiar environments of adult learners involve executing, applying, and prioritizing knowledge, while using knowledge in university settings entails labelling, differentiating, elaborating, and justifying it. (ibid.)

The issue of transfer of learning is also embedded in this category. That is, how the learners can apply their learning in situations other than the context used in the learning process. For adult learners, who typically study alongside their working life, the transfer of learning becomes particularly important. As Bowden and Marton (2004, 25) note: "Anything you learn, you must make use of in other situations. You can never re-enter the very situation which gave birth to learning."

This main category is divided into four sub-categories according to the critical aspects focused on by the learners. That is, what aspects were focal in the learners' awareness, constituting the theme of awareness when experiencing learning as integration of theory and practice. The distinctive ways of experiencing learning ranged from a plain importation of knowledge into one's practice to a compound development of one's professional field. The sub-categories are:

B1. Importing Knowledge into One's Work
B2. Improving One's Performance
B3. Merging Theory and Practice
B4. Developing One's Work

The associated referential and structural aspects of experiencing learning as Integration of Theory and Practice are presented in Table 9.

Table 9. *Referential and structural aspects of the experience of learning as Integration of Theory and Practice*

	CATEGORY B: Learning as Integration of Theory and Practice	
Experience	Referential aspect	Structural aspect
B1	Learning as importing knowledge into one's work	Focus on imparting ideas and knowledge
B2	Learning as improving one's performance	Focus on stylizing changes to performance
B3	Learning as merging theory and practice	Focus on bringing theory and practice into contact
B4	Learning as developing one's work	Focus on bettering and renewing work

7.3.1 Importing Knowledge into One's Work

> I'm bringing the knowledge I got for the use of my work. (Interview 7, Paragraph 142)

In this category, learning as Importing Knowledge into One's Work (B1), the learners are aware of their learning in terms of importing knowledge acquired into one's work environment. When it comes to applying knowledge at a general level, Bowden and Marton (2004, 25) see no reason for dividing situations on the one hand into learning, and on the other hand into application situations. Their point of view is that "every learning situation includes the potential for application (of something learned previously) and every situation of application implies the potential for learning (something new)" (ibid.). This kind of view is perhaps a little idealistic and may not completely represent reality. In this category these two situations are seen by the learners as being apart from each other. The learners felt that they had received a great deal of valuable ideas and knowledge in the learning situations, and that they were able to transfer that knowledge in their work situations (quote below).

> And you can bring here real ideas. (Interview 7, Paragraph 142)

They were also eager to put that knowledge at their colleagues' disposal.

> You certainly see the learning in how I act, how I do, how I bring my new knowledge to the field. (Interview 5, Paragraph 38)

However, this category included no evidence of how the learners actually applied the formal (declarative) knowledge to their practice. The main intention of the learners seemed to be just importing and distributing the knowledge as quickly as possible in their work field, as shown by the quote below.

> So that I have time to bring the idea and information and spread it already before I find the time to ask for permission from the employer. (Interview 5, Paragraph 42)

Actenhagen (1995, 411) has observed that very often, and particularly in the field of teaching and learning (which is comparable to the field of the present research), practitioners refuse to accept new theoretical results, or they convert them in such a way that they lose their original power. According to him (ibid.) this is a sign of the fact that university studies often handle practical problems verbally but not empirically, i.e., they are too concerned with symbolic knowledge neglecting the experiential aspect of them, and so creating difficulties in applying what is learnt.

7.3.2 Improving One's Performance

> You get so much material for various things in your own teaching and overall in being in the work community...(Interview 17, Paragraph 27)

In the category, learning as Improving One's Performance (B2), the learners are aware of their learning in terms of developing their performance in their work field. They model their work after patterns borrowed from their own studies. However, it is also apparent that the learners are likely to seek for ready-to-implement patterns instead of creating new ones by themselves. Marceau (2003, 71) has observed the same tendency. According to his (ibid.) point of view, adult educators (who are comparable to the participants in the present research) who participate in professional development activities tend to ask for hands-on techniques that they can take away and implement immediately with their own students. The quotes below characterise these features of this category.

> Samples for doing tasks and various materials as such... it's easy to revise old material by taking samples from my own studies. Readjust group works, readjust material, self-study material and at least I've gained a lot. (Interview 5, Paragraph 78)

The learners felt satisfied when they received a lot of material for their own teaching as well as for their other activities in the work community in general (quote below).

> ...but of course you get so much material for various things in your own teaching and overall in being in the work community...(Interview 17, Paragraph 27)

As becomes apparent from all three quotes above, in this sub-category the learners do not just transport knowledge (which was the case in the previous, B1, category) but also mould their patterns of acting in order to develop their practices. Therefore, this category might be interpreted as presenting a simple kind of application of what is learnt. However, it is obvious that the learners are likely to only collect and copy best practices from the study materials, and utilise that material unchanged when improving their work performance.

7.3.3 Merging Theory and Practice

> It has been nice to see that there's a theoretical basis to the ways I work. (Interview 10, Paragraph 74)

In this category, Merging Theory and Practice (B3), the learners are aware of their learning in terms of expanded comprehension of one's work by bringing theory and practice into contact, i.e. merging formal (declarative) and practical (procedural) knowledge. The learners' theme of awareness concerning the category of Integration of Theory and Practice has expanded from vague and undifferentiated to a more complex and connected.

In contrast to the previous sub-category (B2), practice is considered here in the light of fusing theory and experience together instead of altering one's external performance. The present category (see also quote below) describes a situation where the learners understand theory through their work and subsequently the theory makes their practice more comprehensible to them.

> I now have a somewhat funny way to act, a bit different. It isn't like I'd go and just do the task, I have some kind of background theory from the university. I've realized it myself, too. (Interview 13, Paragraph 178)

Leinhardt et al. (1995, 158) explain that a true integration of declarative and procedural knowledge is best fostered when university students transform theories for use in practical situations, and accordingly employ their practical knowledge to construct conceptual models. The next quote is a sample of transforming theories for practical situations. It also illustrates the learner's satisfaction when grasping that there exist theoretical explanations concerning their way of acting in practical situations.

> It's quite wonderful to realize that of the things you do at work someone has come up with theories for them. (Interview 3, Paragraph 30)

Bromme and Tillema (1995, 266) claim that becoming professional is not a process of merely substituting theory with experience but a process of fusing theory and experience together. Unlike in the two previous sub-categories (Importing Knowledge into One's Work, B1, and Improving One's Performance, B2) in this category a clear emphasis is placed by the learners on understanding one's work, as mentioned above and further discussed here. This understanding is felt to take place through recognising links between theory and practice i.e. finding connections between one's own way of doing things and the theories behind that practical activity. It might be said that theory and practice here form a sound relationship in which theory generates understanding of practice and vice versa. The two statements below are clear signs of the concordance regarding theory and practice.

> It has been nice to see that there's a theoretical basis to the ways I work. (Interview 10, Paragraph 74)

> Before, always when I did something I always thought how wiser people would do it. And then when I've read theories I could do just like I used to. (Interview 13, Paragraph 182)

The learners also realised that in order to understand one's work better and in order to operate more confidently as professionals, a theoretical framework was required. This contributed to learners' appreciation for theoretical knowledge in general, as is shown in the quote below.

> It's just the theoretical frame of reference and background to this work. Then you have much more secure feeling that you can work especially in your own role. That's really important. When you prepare adult education and various types of services and others you can take into account the theories in that and understand better adult's learning and being a student. (Interview 18, Paragraph 134)

This category comes close to what Bromme and Tillema (1995, 263) call professional knowledge. They (ibid.) define it as "the active-oriented knowledge of practitioners," which "includes not only special information about the facts and proven methods of problem solving, but also information which is required to define and understand the problems a professional is confronted with." The quote below once again points out the necessity and usefulness of theoretical knowledge as it contributes to the solving of practical problems.

> ...some researcher approach... that would be a really important ability in adult education. There's too much of "going and sort of extinguishing the fire". That's... so far from the university world, it's so concrete, but people don't see how it's still related to this theory. That's the problem here. (Interview 11, Paragraph 118)

7.3.4 Developing One's Work

> I shall perhaps be able to do my work better in the future or will be able to do new things. (Interview 17, Paragraph 79)

In this category, Developing One's Work (B4), the learners are aware of their learning in terms of seeing themselves as better able to develop their work and work community than they were before. The learners were not just keen on imparting ideas and knowledge in their work but were also interested in improving their practice. They felt that the studies had contributed to their work by introducing fresh dimensions to it, as becomes evident in the quote below.

> …regarding work, these studies and the way I apply them to the work, they have brought totally different dimensions to it. (Interview 3, Paragraph 102)

At a general level the learners felt that everything they did at work was now improving. They spoke about two types of work development; making their work qualitatively better than it was before and being able to do new things. The quote below provides examples of both of these ways of experiencing learning.

> …I'd say this hasn't given just one, straight tool so that everything goes better now. But this gives me a chance to construct a whole which I can use to do my work in future perhaps better than earlier. Or rather that I can in general do these new things. (Interview 17, Paragraph 79)

To sum it all up, this category is supported by Bromme & Tillema's (1995, 262) suggestion that "professional knowledge is developed as a product of professional action, and it establishes itself through work and performance in the profession,…through the integration, tuning and restructuring of theoretical knowledge to the demands of practical situations and constraints."

Table 10 below summarises the critical aspect of the range of variation in ways of experiencing learning as Integration of Theory and Practice.

Table 10. *The range of variation in ways of experiencing learning as Integration of Theory and Practice*

Themes of expanding awareness	Category			
	Importing Knowledge into One's Work (B1)	Improving One's Performance (B2)	Merging Theory and Practice (B3)	Developing One's Work (B4)
Focus of intention	Imparting ideas and knowledge	Stylising changes to performance	Bringing theory and practice together	Improving and renewing work
Nature of knowledge	Dualistic	Dualistic	Relational	Relational
Type of knowledge	Quantitative	Quantitative	Qualitative	Qualitative
Focus of attention	Sign	Sign	Significant	Significant
Locus of learning	External	External	Internal	Internal

7.4 Self-Regulation of Learning

To be able to control yourself, your time, and to be able to organise things. (Interview 1, Paragraph 108)

The third main category in this research is labelled Self-Regulation of Learning (C). In this category the learners are aware of their learning in terms of triggering, supervising and modifying their learning practices towards their study goals. Moreover, as captured in the title of this chapter, the essence in this category lies in learners' ways of self-regulating their learning processes. This category has no sub-categories. The associated referential and structural aspects of experiencing learning as Self-regulation of Learning are presented in Table 11.

Table 11. *Referential and structural aspects of the experience of learning as Self- Regulation of Learning*

	CATEGORY C: Learning as Self-Regulation of Learning	
	Referential aspect	**Structural aspect**
Experience	Learning as self-regulation of learning	Focus on taking responsibility for one's learning process

The term self-regulation refers to a complex process of interplay, which involves both cognitive self-regulation and motivational self-regulation (e.g. Boekaerts 1997, 161; Sinatra & Pintrich 2003, 2; Ruohotie 2005a, 5). Unlike the two previously discussed main categories (A & B), which manifested the outcomes of learning, this category deals with the learning process.

There are several theoretical perspectives on self-regulation (Schunk 2005, 175). Therefore, before starting to present the empirical details of the present category, I briefly describe the basic features of self-regulation from the point of view of this research.

Self-regulation is in general viewed as a process that can help explain differences in achievement among learners and also improve their achievement (e.g. Schunk 2005, 174 referring to Boekaerts et al., 2000). Luque (2003, 159), for instance, assumes that self-regulation of learning is a necessity for intentional conceptional change to occur. Ruohotie (2000, 1) uses the term self-regulation to refer to "the learner's volitional control and factors affecting his/her motivation." And some precisely claims that it "encompasses the degree that students are meta-cognitively, motivationally and behaviourally active participants in their own learning process" (Zimmerman & Schunk 2001, 5). Pintrich's (2000, 453) characterisation includes elements similar to those above but is still more detailed. According to him (ibid., 453), self-regulation is "an active, constructive process whereby learners set goals for their learning and then attempt to monitor, regulate, and control their cognition, motivation, and behaviour, guided and constrained by their goals and the contextual features in the environment." Regarding the characteristics of a self-regulated learner Zimmerman (2002, 66) points out that they are those who not only have the ability to prepare and take the essential steps in order to learn, but also have the capability to take care of their own monitoring, motivation and feedback processes, both during and after learning.

To summarise, the common feature in self-regulation seems, according to literature, to be the learner's active impact on and participation in his/her learning process. The key components of self-regulation include such processes as goal setting, time management, learning strategies, self-evaluation, self-attributions, seeking help or information, as well as self-motivational beliefs, such as self-efficacy and intrinsic task interest (Zimmerman 2002, 64).

Ruohotie (2000, 11) takes the view that there is a relationship between learners' views of their self-regulation potentials, their self concept and their approach to learning. According to him (ibid.), learners who, in their own opinion, are able to control their learning, are more likely than other learners to use deep information processing approaches. What is said by Ruohotie (ibid.) becomes apparent in the quote of a learner below.

> I don't even want to take it easy. Why would I scratch the surface of the program? So that I'd be in it just for fun. No, I don't want that. When you do it you do it. You give it your all and have fun in other places. (Interview 5, Paragraph 190)

Motivation plays a crucial role in self-regulated learning. It is primarily concerned with an individual's pre-decisional state, that is, what affects a decision to act (Beairsto & Ruohotie 2003, 121) (in the context of this research it refers to what affects learners' decision to study at a university). In a motivational phase the learners are still doubtful whether or not and which kind of target to commit themselves to (Järvenoja et al. 2005, 467). The importance of motivation is clearly expressed in the quote below with one learner feeling his/her own motivation and enthusiasm forming the preconditions for learning.

> I believe that... in adult education it's your own motivation and enthusiasm, they're the starting points for studying. (Interview 15, Paragraph 42)

In addition to motivation volition is also considered to be a fundamental part of self-regulation (see e.g. Pintrich & Ruohotie 2000). Informally, volition is taken to mean (Corno 1993, 14) strength or will with weakness as its opposite. Corno (1994, 229) identifies the term more explicitly as a "tendency to maintain focus and effort towards goals despite distractions."

Volition is concerned with such notions as persistence, will to learn, effort, intrinsic regulation, self evaluation as well as different control strategies (e.g., allocation and control of resources) (Beairsto & Ruohotie 2003, 121; Ruohotie 2000, 3). The notion "will to learn" is taken by Van Eekelen, Vermunt and Boshuizen (in press), to refer to a psychological state in which the learner has a desire to learn. Regarding the temporality of volition Beairsto et al. (2003, 121) note that it is concerned primarily with a post-decisional state of learning, that is, with what affects follow-through on a decision once it is made (in the context of this research it means what affects follow-through on a decision to study at a university). Järvenoja and Järvelä (2005,

467) concur with Beairsto et al. (ibid) in that volition is primarily needed in the execution phase of the learning, when motivation and goal commitment are already established, but the learner must still sustain and support the decisions made. On the other hand Van Eekelen et al. (in press), stress that the will to learn must exist before engaging in the actual learning process. In the quote below the learner argues powerfully for the necessity of the will to learn in a learning process. The same quote also shows the learner's tendency to attribute lack of will to learn.

> I wish that the will to learn would never extinguish, because it's the absolute prerequisite. It's the first prerequisite for learning that you want to learn. If you don't, you'll find 150 explanations for no need to learn and why that program is not good or not suited for me or not giving me the things I need. (Interview 15, Paragraph 110)

In self-regulated learning process learning is viewed as an activity that students do for themselves in a proactive manner (Zimmerman 2002, 65). The next two quotes below are evidence of learners' proactive strategies to control their learning. The temporal aspect of self-regulation also becomes apparent in the same accounts. In the course of their studies, the learners had become more skilled at allocating their resources, particularly that of time, as well as maintaining their efforts towards the goals.

> …to control yourself, control your time, all these kinds of things, to be able to organise things. These have developed really well in about half a year, I'm able to take care of all these things. (Interview 1, Paragraph 108)

> …at first I did it all, in that sense you burn yourself out. But now I've learned to do timetables and stick to them. (Interview 2, Paragraph 54)

Volitional control has mainly to do with self- and task-management when trying to reach the goals, as suggested by Ruohotie (2000, 9). Volitional processes help the learners complete the tasks needed to reach their goals (Järvenoja et al. 2005, 467). The following two quotes are intended to illustrate what volitional control concerning self-management (the strength to start and keep going) and task-management (do it, do it at once without delay) in study situations actually mean from the learners' point of view.

> I've also learned that when you manage to start and do the reward is quite good or good in relation to how much I've worked. (Interview 6, Paragraph 90)

> I've learned that you have to do all things at once …If I do something I see that a thing should be done. That means it must be done now. And then it's done. Some homework or things like that, when you have

> them and there's a moment they need to be done, you'll do them right away and don't leave them undone for several weeks and then have to think about them. (Interview 13, Paragraph 190)

Volitional control also includes (e.g. Ruohotie 2000, 9) such elements as arranging the learning situations so that learning is easier and more enjoyable as well as seeking assistance from peers. Both of these aspects of volitional control are illustrated in the next two quotes. The same quotes also show the role of emotions in a learning process. They may inhibit or promote actions towards the goals (Järvenoja et al. 2005, 467). Self-regulated learners are not only more likely to succeed academically but also to view their futures optimistically (Zimmerman 2002, 66).

> ...there's also somewhat a sharing of burden with other students. And you realize it's all not so serious. That this life is just life, nothing more serious...and this studying isn't so difficult if you want to succeed and learn. (Interview 5, Paragraph 198)

In connection with the present category, aspects of self-efficacy also emerged from the learners' experiences. At a general level self-efficacy refers to "one's capabilities to organise and execute courses of action required to manage prospective situations" (Bandura 1995, 2). In learning, self-efficacy beliefs mean the personal capability to learn, and the outcome expectations concerning that learning (Zimmerman 2002, 68 referring to Bandura 1997). Therefore one's personal efficacy also determines whether actions (like learning) will be initiated, how much effort will be spent on it, and for how long actions will be sustained in case of obstacles and discouraging experiences (Bandura 1977, 191). All in all, self-efficacy has a prominent role in learning because, as assumed by Bandura (in press referring to Bandura 1997), belief in one's efficacy is a core resource in personal development and change. The following quote below includes an example of how efficacy beliefs shape individuals' outcome expectations, i.e. whether they expect their efforts to produce favourable outcomes or adverse ones.

> ... I've regarded this studying in the university somehow to be in much higher level. When I'm in here myself this isn't so terrible that I thought it to be. I can even keep up with it. (Interview 13, Paragraph 146)

Moreover, efficacy beliefs determine how people view opportunities and obstacles. Bandura (in press) explains that people who have low self-efficacy beliefs are easily convinced of the uselessness of effort when facing difficulties. As a consequence they quickly give up trying. On the other hand, people with high efficacy beliefs see obstacles as "surmountable by improvement of self-regulatory skills and persevering effort" (ibid.). They continue in the face of difficulties and remain strong in adversity (ibid.). What is suggested above by Bandura is evidenced in the two example quotes below. It also appears that a self-regulated learner has a range of solutions for altering his/her performance if obstacles are encountered (as stated in the first quote).

> This studying is nice in that way too, …it has given me confirmation that things don't always go so well. And it's good if it in time to time goes well. There's always some means to fix it. (Interview 13, Paragraph 174)

> Of course the tasks are laborious when you wrestle with them, but you have to remember that studying is your own choice. (Interview 2, Paragraph 170)

Self-efficacy beliefs are also influenced by emotional states (e.g. Usher & Pajares 2006, 127). They influence (Bandura, in press) whether individuals sense reality optimistically or pessimistically, i.e. in self-enhancing or self-debilitating ways. Therefore, efficacy beliefs also affect the quality of emotional life and vulnerability to stress and depression (ibid.), as becomes visible from the first quote above as well as from the next ones below.

> …when you complete some assignment it's a good feeling that you have surpassed the thresholds you have done. (Interview 2, Paragraph 122)

> … I'm able to do this kind of degree, I can do that, too. But in a way it's mostly that I feel it myself, I can learn all these new things. (Interview 2, Paragraph 130)

Bouffard et al. (1995) have observed that those learners who engage in self-regulated learning deliberately plan each step of their learning process, select strategies to actualise their plans, and in addition control and evaluate the effectiveness of those strategies. Just the same tendency became apparent from learners' descriptions related to this category.

7.5   Professional Growth and Development

> I'm growing out of my current job description. (Interview 12, Paragraph 114)

In this Professional Growth and Development (D) category the learners are aware of their learning in terms of enhancing their capabilities as professionals. This category did not include any sub-categories. The associated referential and structural aspects of experiencing learning as Professional Growth and Development are presented in Table 12.

Table 12. *Referential and structural aspects of the experience of learning as Professional Growth and Development*

CATEGORY D: Learning as Professional Growth and Development	
Referential aspect	**Structural aspect**
Experience Learning as professional growth and development	Focus on enhancing capabilities as a professional

Van Eekelen et al. (in press) make the point that although continued professional development may be a necessity among adults, it cannot, however, be taken for granted. Based on the results of this research I agree with what is said by Van Eekelen et al. (ibid.). It was noticed that not all of the participants of the research seemed to engage their ways of experiencing learning in professional growth and development, although that was one of the aims of the studies.

Various definitions have been evinced for the terms professional growth and professional development. Sometimes these two terms are seen as equivalent while on other occasions they have different meanings. With regard to the term growth in general, Pring (2005, 82) explains it in the following way: "Growth is not unfolding of what is already there. Rather it is gradual expansion of one's experience and understanding through the interaction between a person… and social and cultural environment in which he finds himself." The components of temporality and interaction of growth are emphasised in this definition.

The term professional development is defined by the thesaurus of the Educational Resources Information Center (ERIC) as "activities to enhance professional career growth." The same kind of idea is evinced by Ruohotie (1999, 8), suggesting that professional development includes all developmental functions which are directed towards the maintenance and enhancement of professional competence.

Beairsto (1996, 94), for one, points out that the terms professional growth and professional development should not be confused but rather seen as complementary processes. According to him (ibid.), the difference between the two terms is that professional growth likely describes the broadening of expertise or area of knowledge or ability in relation to a known domain, whereas professional development illustrates the process of extending into qualitatively new areas of knowledge or ability. Beairsto's view of growth, "broadening of expertise or area of knowledge or ability", concurs well with that of Pring, "gradual expansion of one's experience and understanding", mentioned above. Regarding professional development Cranton and King (2003, 33) agree with Beairsto's view, asserting that a meaningful professional development must go further than just learning a new trick.

In this research the terms professional growth and professional development are seen as overlapping, although the differences between them are understood. It is believed that, as a consequence of studying, the learners both grow and develop as professionals (or then not). It is also thought here that the studies taken at a university are meant to represent some kind of a professional development intervention for them. Therefore the term development is used here to refer to both of these concepts. The terms competence and professional, although related to the present topic but not direct key points of the category, will not be discussed here.

On a general level the learners found that their studies at the university involved features that fostered their professional development. The impression of development, for example, was expressed by one learner in the following manner:

> I've noticed that I can learn and evolve and develop myself. You study quite much for yourself. (Interview 2, Paragraph 22)

The studies and professional development were seen by the learners to be related to their career development. They were particularly taken as a necessary option for a future career, as is evidenced in the quote below.

> Could studying also somehow secure my later work career? If it could be described by development. (Interview 6, Paragraph 106)

In this category the learners expressed having also experienced a kind of renewal as a consequence of studying. This might refer to some kind of professional updating process in which the studies are seen as a good way to avoid professional obsolescence (see. e.g. Ruohotie 1996, 1999) (quote below).

> ...if I wasn't in TUKEVA I don't know where I could've looked for and gained the variety of regeneration. (Interview 18, Paragraph 166)

Professional development was also taken as a way to relax and to avoid stress. In connection with this topic one student, for example, reported that

> ...I like to study. It's my lifeline. It's a way for me to the road to development. It prevents exhaustion. I think it's pretty good to say that you don't need the road of a fighter when you choose the road of a developer. (Interview 5, Paragraph 70)

Learning involved in professional growth and development takes many forms (e.g. Ruohotie 1999, 20). Cranton and King (2003), for instance, prefer transformative learning for that purpose. They (ibid., 32) assert that transformative learning, when examining one's practice critically, and thereby acquiring alternative ways of understanding what one does, must be a goal of professional development (Cranton et al. 2003, 32). The quote below seems to indicate the learner's attempt to transform, to find alternative perspectives in addition to what is officially required for the course exam.

> It's more important for me to learn a little more and different way than what a degree just gives or demands. I'll selfishly choose my own development first. And hopefully that fills the degree areas. (Interview 5, Paragraph 158)

From the experiences of learners it also became apparent that professional development can be a way to empower individuals as professionals (see e.g. Lawler & King 2003). According to Niemi (2002, 8), empowerment means that a person has an improved ability or power to manage personal capacities. The next two quotes imply views of empowerment in learners' ways of acting as professionals as a consequence of studies. The learners felt more confident in their work.

> I've got a kind of confidence in what I'm doing. Before, always when I did something I always thought how wiser people would do it. And then when I've read them I could do just like I used to. (Interview 13, Paragraph 182)

> Now you have a feeling of control in the work and don't feel helpless all time and think you aren't able to and can't do it. Studying always brings... professional resources. (Interview 18, Paragraph 166)

Both of the quotes above, as well as the next one, are descriptions of a successful professional updating process. Ruohotie (1999, 18) writes that this kind of process "leads to an accentuated knowledge of self as the agent of one's own career and makes future learning cycles more likely." The quote below visibly shows that a proactive approach towards professional development enables the learner to be an agent in preparing to meet his/her new professional challenges. An outcome of successful professional updating process was, for instance, expressed by one learner: "I'm not with those who are left behind."

> I think I'm not the only one who thinks that studying is for quite many a saviour regarding working life. You get renewed and believe in yourself and get confidence and perhaps also more self-respect. So that I'm not with those who are left behind but in the frontlines... And you must learn if you want to mature... to a wider outlook in the teacher's profession...(Interview 5, Paragraph 198)

When specifying environmental prerequisites for professional development Ruohotie (1999, 11-12) explains that ideal situations are those in which the individual has opportunities for ongoing growth and development alongside his/her work. In such situations one's tasks and positions form a continuous course which one feels is advancing, as seemed to be the case with the learner quoted above. Ruohotie (1999, 11-12) continues that in practice, however, growth often halts or gets stuck at some point (as seems to the case with the quote below), with the result that the handling of tasks becomes a routine. The learner felt that as a consequence of professional growth and development he/she is growing out of his/her current job and is actively searching for new career prospects.

> You're able to talk with the superiors in a different level. But on the other hand, I've noticed that the gap to the team mates has perhaps increased. Even though I've consciously tried to avoid that... We've talked in work that I'm growing out of my current job description. But that doesn't mean I'd leave the workplace. We've talked we'd see if there would be some other tasks. But it does mean that my job description has to change. (Interview 12, Paragraph 114)

Cranton et al. (2003, 33) stress that when dealing with the issue of professional development it is important to involve the learner as a whole person. This means that one needs to take into account the learner's values, beliefs, and assumptions about his/her profession and ways of seeing the world. This view concurs well with the feelings of the learner in the next quote. Regarding professional development Cranton et al. (2003, 34) state that it brings habits of mind into awareness and allows one to examine critically what he/she believes and values as a professional. As a consequence of this process, professional development opens up alternatives and introduces new ways of thinking about one's profession. (Cranton & King 2003, 34-35.) The features of professional development described above by Cranton et al. are evidenced in the quote below. The same quote also brings together the main features of the category Professional Growth and Development.

> I've learned a plethora of things. I can't single it out but I feel I've become a totally different person. This whole process continues all the time. Now I don't anymore think I wouldn't know about anything. The more you know, the more you suffer but I feel I have a totally different way to think and different scheme of things and I pay attention to different things. On the other hand, I realize I've become more critical towards many kinds of things. I don't really put up with general remarks. I've noticed that I start to ask questions; what do you mean and what way, and who said so and when and to whom. Our instructor said that you're now entering a road with no return. You won't ever think about things the way you think now. And I totally subscribe to that. It's reflected to everything you do and think, you have so different ways to think. (Interview 15, Paragraph 110)

And finally Table 13 summarises TUKEVA students' qualitatively different ways of experiencing learning and simultaneously **answers the first research question: What kind of variation is there in adult learners' ways of experiencing their learning at a university?**

Table 13. *Summary of the variations in the ways of experiencing learning*

Categories	Descriptions	Sample statements
Learning as Cognitive Phases of Learning (A)		
Aggregation of Knowledge (A1)	Learners are aware of their learning in terms of adding new, quantifiable knowledge to their previous knowledge.	...I've received so much new information... sure, I'm getting new information all the time... I can't yet really classify it...who can then apply the information... I don't yet know where I could at least use it so much... you know so many things but real life is something very different.
Memorisation (A2)	The learners are aware of their learning in terms of keeping knowledge in mind, i.e. being able to memorise (remember) things from the studies / study material.	...repeating old things... it came back to me... I have to memorise the information right away or I lose it... to pass that test... and get a degree...
Transforming Knowledge into Meaning (A3)	Learners are aware of their learning in terms of making meaning of phenomena.	If you don't learn by heart you understand things you haven't ever studied... you finally find something familiar... I have a view of my own now... you see contexts in a different way... an ability to structure and see things in a new way... you're able to connect the things... I've started to see entities rather than details. ... to be more critical towards all kinds of things....
Changed Views of Reality (A4)	The learners are aware of their learning in terms of changed views of reality.	...this change in my way of thinking... you see things differently... the composure and will and ability to see things from many perspectives... to be more critical towards all kinds of things... it doesn't seen to fit to old frameworks... another view of myself... it's reflected in all I do or think
Learning as Integration of Theory and Practice (B)		
Importing Knowledge into One's Work (B1)	The learners are aware of their learning in terms of transferring knowledge acquired into their work environment.	It's possible to bring your ideas to the work... I'm bringing the knowledge I get for the use of my field... there are places where you can check the information, you easily get information for the work
Improving One's Performance (B2)	The learners are aware of their learning in terms of improving their work performance.	...models for your actions... you can make something new from your old materials by taking patterns from your own studies... you get so much material for various things in your teaching and in general to your activities in the work community
Merging Theory and Practice (B3)	The learners are aware of their learning in terms of expanded comprehension of one's work through the combining of theory and practice, i.e. merging formal (declarative) knowledge and practical (procedural) knowledge.	I love to see that someone has invented theories about the things you do at work... that there's a theory for the way you work... I've learned to structure my work and the thoughts in it... understand better adult learning and being a student.

Developing One's Work B4)	The learners are aware of their learning in terms of seeing themselves as more capable than before to develop their work and work community.	... given me tools for my work, a way to develop my work... brought whole new dimensions to my work... I'm perhaps able to do my work better in the future or can do new things.

Learning as Self-Regulation of Learning (C)

Self-Regulation of Learning	The learners are aware of their learning in terms of triggering, supervising and modifying their learning practices in accordance with their study goals.	...in order to learn you must have the will to learn... your own motivation and enthusiasm are the bases... to be able to control yourself, your time, to be able to organise things... you surpass yourself... when you have the strength to start and do it, you get a good reward... when you achieve the goals you've made yourself it's a nice feeling... you feel good to have solved this one, too

Learning as Professional Growth and Development (D)

Professional Growth and Development	The learners are aware of their learning in terms of enhancing their capabilities as professionals.	...I've noticed that you learn and develop... studies are a gate to some road of development...I've searched for and found many kinds of renewal... there's more firmness in what you do... it has boosted me as an instructor and teacher... I'm not with those who are left behind... I'm growing out of my current job description

The answer to the second research question: **What kind of a holistic view can be constituted from adult learners' various ways of experiencing their learning at a university** is given in the form of an outcome space. The outcome space is presented in Figure 6 and further discussed in the next chapter (Chapter 8) in relation to the principal findings of the research.

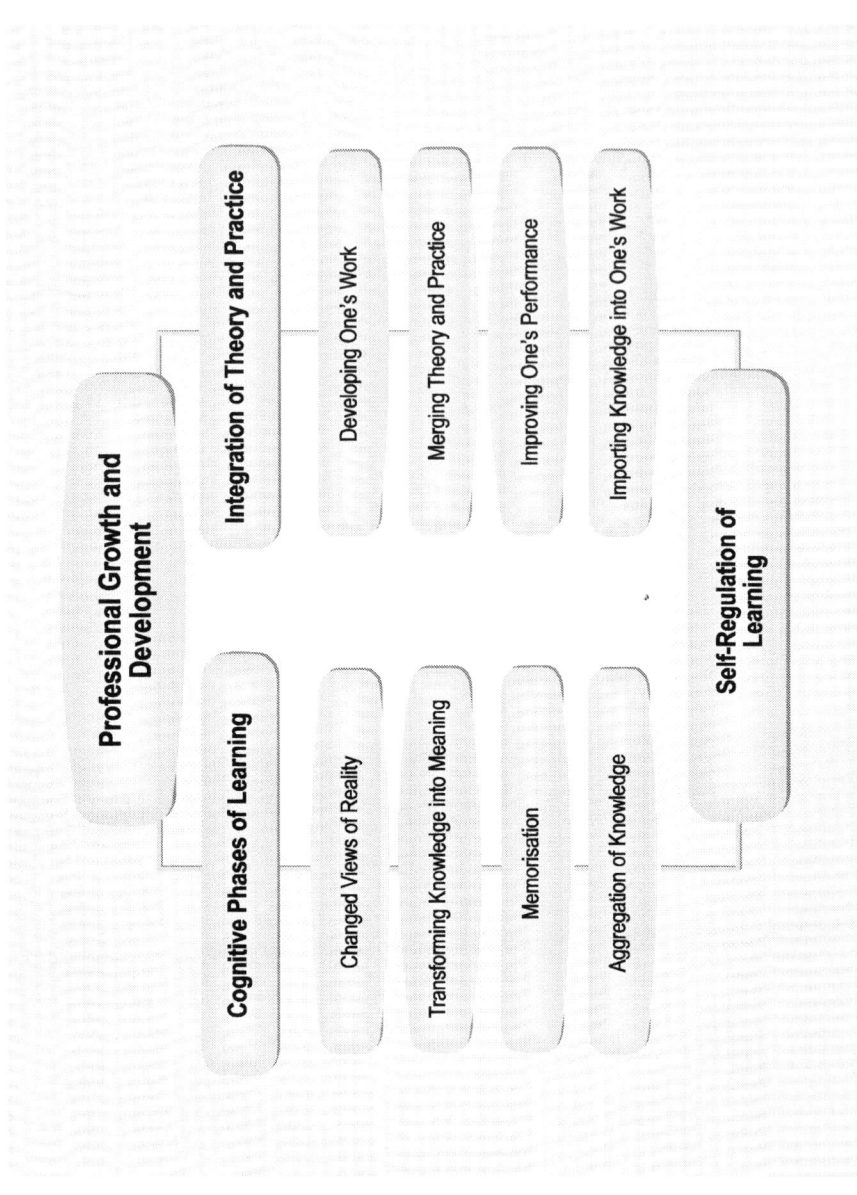

Figure 6. The outcome space of adult learners' various ways of experiencing learning

7.6 Phenomenography as a Research Approach

This section answers the third research question: What kind of research approach is phenomenography in investigating adult learners' experiences of their learning at a university? I will first briefly summarise the main principles of the approach in order to refresh the reader's memory regarding the core ideas behind it. Thereafter, I continue with my notions using phenomenography as a research approach.

The phenomenographic research approach is characterised by an interest in discovering the qualitatively different ways in which a particular phenomenon (here learning) is experienced (Marton, Watkins & Tang 1997, 44) by certain group of people. The ultimate aim is to constitute from those experiences a limited number of internally related and hierarchical categories (Pritchard, Heatly & Trigwell 2005) which, as a result of the research, form an outcome space (Marton 2000, 105). This outcome space provides an empirically based description of the phenomenon as experienced by the participants of the research. The description points to a collective level, as it represents variation in experiences across the participants. (e.g. Marton, Watkins & Tang 1997, 44.)

In recent years, the phenomenographic research approach has shifted its emphasis from methodological to more theoretical concerns with regard to learning. Following the idea of the field of consciousness evinced by Gurwitsch (1964), Marton and Booth (1997) recently put forward a theory of human awareness. In this theory Marton and Booth argue that a way of experiencing a phenomenon can be described in terms of how the human being's awareness is structured.

When the phenomenographic view of learning is compared to other contemporary views, the former, due to its different epistemological stance, differs from learning theories rooted in psychology, cognitive science, and constructivism (e.g. Linder & Marshall 2003, 272). As stated by Watkins (2000, 104), "phenomenography views individuals as bearers of different experiences rather than as behaviourist impersonators, bearers of mental representations, or individual or social actors." In other words, phenomenography does not portray learning in terms of mental models or as something that is created outside of a person in social practices. Instead, it takes advantage of Brentano's (1973) notion of intentionality to characterise the non-dualist nature of experience (Linder & Marshall 2003, 272).

According to non-dualism, experience is seen as an internal relationship constituted between a human being (experiencer) and reality (experienced) (Marton & Booth 1997, 108). This non-dualist nature of experience is the most essential feature of phenomenography and facilitates a research perspective known as the second order perspective (Linder & Marshall 2003, 272). In this research the second order perspective means that instead of having studied learning per se, I have studied participants' descriptions of their learning.

When assessing what kind of research approach phenomenography is for investigating adult learners' experiences of their learning I must reflect upon the requirements I set when determining an appropriate approach for my study. I stipulated (in Section 5.1.1), that the research approach should

- allow adult learners' individual and collective voices to be heard
- allow access to adult learners' lived experience concerning their learning
- allow variations in adult learners' lived experience to come to light
- allow description of the adult learners' experiences of learning
- allow an holistic view of the phenomena of experiencing learning
- contribute to the research and practice of adults' learning

My overall view is that the above requirements were adequately met using the phenomenographic approach. As the phenomenographer relies on language as a source of empirical evidence, I gained access to the adult learner's learning experiences through spoken and written data. There was a crucial challenge to get the participants to describe their learning experiences in a manner that allowed variation to occur. The categorisation I constituted from the data allowed both individual and collective voices to be heard and learners' diverse learning experiences to be revealed.

The greatest benefit of the phenomenographic research approach I perceived was that it appeared to enable me to reveal the variations in the experiences of learning among a chosen group of participants. It moreover allowed me to define the relationships between those varying experiences, and therefore organise them into the holistic form of an outcome space. The last requirement regarding the contribution of this study to the research and practice of adult learners' learning is elaborated in the next chapter (Chapter 8). Thus the phenomenographic approach appeared to satisfy the requirements I set for the research.

However, in order not to give too rosy a picture of the phenomenographic research endeavour, I must admit that in the course of the research I was confronted with tricky questions more than once. Time and again I felt confused by several ideas behind phenomenography and even felt overwhelmed by all the demanding principles underlying this approach. Two such cases are described below. As the following discussion shows, other researchers have encountered similar problems with phenomenography.

For example, when familiarising myself with the phenomenographic research approach there was overall confusion about the fundamental unit of the research. Earlier, a way of experiencing was introduced by Marton and Booth (1997, 98) as a basic unit of investigation. However, more recently Marton and Pong (2005, 336) have proposed that it is rather a conception which is the basic unit. Such terms as ways of conceptualising, ways of seeing, ways of apprehending, ways of understanding, and so on have been used for the same purpose. Thus, the range of terms for a basic unit of investigation in phenomenography is extensive. Regrettably the terms in themselves are not comparable to each other.

However, this terminological problem has recently been recognised by Marton and Pong (ibid.). They have also clarified their rationale: "The reason for using so many different synonyms is that although none of them corresponds completely to what we have in mind, they all do to a certain extent." In addition, they admit that "it is perfectly clear that conceptualising is not identical with experiencing…" because the researcher "…can discern and focus upon conceptual feature just as one can discern and focus on sense-related features" (ibid.). In the former case it is conceptualising that is the basic unit and in the latter experiencing. Thus, my using the term a way of experiencing as a basic unit in this research concurs well with Marton and Pong's clarification above.

As discussed above, phenomenography draws on and complements the cognitivist's and individual constructivist's concern with the inner content of experience, as well as the behaviourist's and social constructivist's concern with the outer structuring of experience (Watkins 2000, 104). However, I argue that it is problematic or hardly possible to deal with learning without considering the psychological and cognitive aspects of the human mind. From my point of view, as human beings we are first and foremost reasonable creatures, and interpret our experiences by aware thinking, and consequently make sense of reality by thinking about it (unlike animals, which act instinctively). I therefore agree with Tao (2002, 115) that a constructivist view of learning and phenomenographic theories of variation and structure of awareness could have complementary and collaborative roles to play in learning.

Säljö (1996, 28) queries the same issue by asking: "How can we possibly talk about learning as a change between conceptions... and yet not use a psychological language or point to psychological phenomena...? What could be gained and why should it be desirable to talk about the phenomenon such as these without using a language that points to events and experiences of a psychological nature?" In the same line Latomaa (2005, 46) suggests that phenomenography, as a research approach which concentrates on investigating human being's subjective experiences, can be equated with psychology.

Actually, similar ideas have recently been evinced by some other researchers. For example, Linder and Marshall (2003) have explored the links between the characterisations of learning stemming from Marton and Booth's (1997) phenomenographic research orientation and Schön's (e.g. 1987) reflection-in-action. They argue that these two parallels open up new ways of viewing Schön's work, which, in turn, facilitate a theoretical development for a phenomenographic view of learning. (Linder and Marshall 2003, 282.) Cornu (2005), for one, suggests linking Jarvis' (2004) model of learning with phenomenography. She considers that, given Marton and Booth's (1997) focus on awareness and Jarvis's own understanding of the role of consciousness, learning continues to be portrayed from a highly cognitive perspective.

The above discussion about confusion in the phenomenographic research approach, however, does not mean that I advocate abandoning it. On the contrary, as has become evident in the research report, the phenomenographic research approach has provided me with a fresh theoretical and methodological framework for conducting the present research on learning. As an evolving approach, phenomenography has its shortcomings, but this sets researchers a task to reveal the weak points step by step and to eliminate them.

In conclusion, when estimating what kind of approach phenomenography is for investigating adult learners' experiences of their learning, my judgement is supported by Cornu's (2005) statement: "While the model remains an imperfect vehicle in attempting to portray the intricacies of human learning, it nonetheless provides a structure by which scholarly understanding of the processes can advance."

8 DISCUSSION AND CONCLUSIONS

In this chapter I will bring to a close my challenging journey of exploration of a phenomenographic research project on university adult learners' learning experiences. The chapter starts by highlighting the principal findings established in the course of the investigation. The category-specific results are presented in more detail in the relevant passages in Chapter 7, in connection with each separate category. After forming a comprehensive picture of the findings, the contribution of the research is assessed, likewise its implications for educational research and practice. Finally, the chapter outlines challenges for further research occasioned by the present findings.

8.1 Principal Findings

The purpose of this research was to create new knowledge and understanding of adult learners' learning at a university and to promote methods for investigating that learning. The rationale for the research came from Marton and Booth's (1997, 111) notion that in order to make sense of how people handle problems, situations and the world, one has to understand the ways in which they experience these things. From the perspective of successful learning at a university the previous statement demands a better understanding the learners' various experiences of learning. This research was also prompted by Biggs (1999) assumption that experience of learning affects approaches to learning which in turn affect (Trigwell & Prosser 1996) learning outcomes. It was consequently thought by the present researcher that finding out more about adult learners' experiences of learning might help learners and pedagogues improve the quality of learning.

The research used a phenomenographic research approach, more specifically that called "new phenomenography", both as an empirical research methodology and as a theoretical perspective on learning. The main principle in phenomenography is that a particular phenomenon (here learning) can be experienced in a limited number of qualitatively varying ways and the various ways of experiencing can be expressed in a hierarchy of increasing complexity (Marton & Booth, 1997). This is what the phenomenographer pursues in his/her research endeavour. Consequently, this research addressed the following three questions: **What kind of variation is there in adult learners' ways of experiencing their learning at a university? What kind of a holistic view can be constituted from adult learners' various ways of experiencing their learning at a university? What kind of research approach is phenomenography in investigating adult learners' experiences of their learning at a university?**

From the theoretical viewpoint, the most important results of the research are the findings of learners' qualitatively varying ways of experiencing their learning. As is customary in phenomenography, these findings of the research are presented as a holistic set of varying degrees of categories of description (see Figure 5 in Chapter 7) in an outcome space (see Figure 6 in Chapter 7). This outcome space is the overall main product of the research and answers the first two research questions. The outcome space represents a kind of a collective anatomy of the structure of learners' awareness showing the key aspects of different ways in which learning can be experienced and their relationships with each other.

In general, the research shows that the adult learners' qualitative ways of experiencing learning varied from simple to more sophisticated. They ranged from experiences that learning is an isolated collection of knowledge fragments, through to experiences that learning is an inseparable part of learners' professional growth and development. According to the findings, the Professional Growth and Development category as the most complete way of experiencing learning seemed to involve cognitive, practical and self-regulative aspects of learning.

It should be noted here, as was also mentioned earlier in this report, that this research was interested in learners' perceptions of their learning experiences and therefore did not even try to distinguish actual (real) learning, in the sense of grades or level of thinking skills, from learning experienced. Because of the second order perspective taken in a phenomenographic research, I do not claim to have investigated what there is in the reality but I do claim to have investigated what there is in adult learners' experiences of reality (see also van Eekelen et al. 2005, 464). And therefore, the findings of the research do not indicate how much someone has learned or how correct (in the sense of right or wrong) someone's learning has been. Instead they rather describe a structure of awareness of experiencing of learning (see Marton & Booth 1997) among adult learners. Thus, based on the idea of the anatomy of awareness, the research also revealed that there are, among adult learners at a university, variations in the structures of awareness with regard to the phenomenon of learning.

Four qualitatively distinct main categories in ways of experiencing learning as an adult university learner were formed from the interview data. The categories were differentiated from each other by variation along four dimensions: cognition, practice, self-regulation, and professional growth and development. Learning was correspondingly experienced as:

A. Cognitive Phases of learning
B. Integration of Theory and Practice
C. Self-Regulation of Learning
D. Professional Growth and Development.

The first main category, learning as Cognitive Phases of Learning (A), focuses on what is happening within the minds of the learners. According to this view, learners' ways of experiencing learning seem to be just a matter of pure cognition. In the second main category, learning as Integration of Theory and Practice (B), the learners are aware of their learning in terms of combining theory learned in university studies with their everyday work. The key idea behind this category lies in learners' ways of seeing their learning through the eyes of professionals in action. The third main category in this research is labelled learning as Self-Regulation of Learning (C). In this category the learners are aware of their learning in terms of triggering and supervising their learning as well as modifying their learning practices towards their study goals. Its essence here lies in learners deliberately taking responsibility for their own learning. And finally, in the Professional Growth and Development category (D), which stands at the top of the categorisation, the learners are aware of their learning in terms of enhancing their capabilities as professionals.

In addition, the findings revealed that not many adult learners attached their learning experiences to those categories that denoted the most complete ways of experiencing learning; they are Changed Views of Reality (A4), Developing One's Work (B4), Professional Growth and Development (D) and Self-Regulation of Learning (C). Instead, numerous learners' experiences fell into the categories that indicated less advanced ways of learning: Aggregating of Knowledge (A1), Memorising (A2), and Importing Knowledge into One's Work (B1). Marton et al. (1993) have also paid attention to the issue that being able to see things differently or changing as a person is not typical for students at a university. However, the aim of the university studies is the opposite.

When the findings of this research are compared with the findings of other phenomenographic studies on the phenomenon of learning, interesting similarities as well as differences emerge. However, it should be noted here that in the studies reported below the participants have mainly been mainstream university students but not adults taking degree programmes alongside their normal work. Furthermore, the investigations have been conducted in different cultural settings, thus the results are naturally not directly comparable with the findings of the present research.

Perhaps the best known categories of description concerning learning experiences are those which were initially identified by Säljö (1979, 1982) and Giorgi (1986) and thereafter revised by Marton, DallAlba and Beaty (1993) when investigating the conceptions of learning among students at Britain's Open University. Learning was conceptualized by them as: 1) increasing one's knowledge, 2) memorising and reproducing, 3) applying, 4) understanding, 5) seeing something in a different way and 6) changing as a person. The first three categories depict learning as a reproduction of information while the last three describe learning as primarily seeking meaning. (Marton et al. 1993). In the present research three additional categories were found, two of which (B and D) placed strong emphasis on practice and professional-bound learning, and one category (C) taking responsibility for one's learning.

The above categorisation (Marton et al. 1993) has subsequently been identified in several other studies. For instance, Boulton-Lewis, Wilss and Lewis (2001) investigated university students during the first two years of their degree courses in three Australian universities. The sample comprised 17 students studying various degrees. Ages ranged from 18 to 48 years. The core conceptions of learning among those students were: 1) acquisition, 2) understanding, 3) personal growth, 4) see something differently, and 5) change in thinking and understanding. As one can easily recognise, the categories seem in many respects to be similar to those found by Marton et al. (1993). The present research involved a growth dimension as well, but here it was more from a professional perspective.

In order to see conceptions of learning from the perspective of educators, Prosser, Trigwell and Taylor (1994) studied how university teachers see learning. They identified five categories which were also interestingly quite consistent with those of the students' conceptions discussed above: 1) accumulating more information to satisfy external demands, 2) acquiring concepts to satisfy external demands, 3) acquiring concepts to satisfy internal demands, 4) conceptual development to satisfy internal demands, and 5) conceptual change to satisfy internal demands.

Tynjälä (1997, 1999b), for one, examined 31 first-year educational psychology university students pursuing courses in different learning environments. As a result of her research, seven categories of description of the students' conceptions of the learning process were identified; learning as 1) an externally determined event/process, 2) a developmental process, 3) student activity, 4) strategies/styles/approaches, 5) information processing, 6) interactive process, and 7) creative process. It is, however important to note that the previous categories concern the students' descriptions of the learning process and not the products or definitions of learning. According to Tynjälä (ibid.), this explains the absence of categories, like increasing one's knowledge, memorising and reproducing, understanding ect., which were included in other researchers' categorisations (e.g. Säljö 1979, 1982; Marton et al. 1993; Boulton-Lewis et al. 2001; Prosser et al. 1994), as well as in the categorisation of the present research.

To sum up, the conceptions and experiences of learning discussed above are not all identical with those found in this research. However, they are not completely different either, but rather seem to be to some extent overlapping with the present findings. In fact, the learning as Cognitive Phases of Learning category resembles the categorisation initiated by Marton et al.

(1993), however, with the exception that an application aspect is absent here. On the other hand, the present research involves a category, termed Integration of Theory and Practice, which can more or less be thought as a substitute for the application category. According to the empirical evidence, there was no doubt of the existence of this type of category. Therefore, it would have been unfair to submit those work-related learning experiences to just the notion of application. It should also be remembered here that variation is what a phenomenographer strives for. Furthermore, when comparing the present results with others mentioned, this research identifies two additional categories, learning as Self-Regulation of Learning, and learning as Professional Growth and Development, which have not been mentioned in other comparable studies.

The principal findings can be summarised as follows:

- There are variations in adult learners' ways of experiencing their learning, and consequently in their structure of awareness concerning learning in a university setting.
- The outcome space shows that adult ways of experiencing learning are a combination of cognition, practice, professional growth and development, and self-regulation of learning.
- The findings indicate that the different ways of experiencing learning form a hierarchy of increasing completeness.
- The findings indicate that the most complete category of adult learners' learning at a university in this study consists of being capable of changing his/her views of reality, develop his/her work, grow and develop as a professional and self-regulate his/her learning.
- The findings indicate that only a few learners were attached to the most complete ways of experiencing learning.

In conclusion, this research has shown that there are notable variations in the ways the adult learners experience their learning. As its main result, the research constituted a holistic portrayal, in the form of phenomenographic outcome space, of adult learners' ways of experiencing learning in the university setting. This holistic portrayal indicates that adults' learning comprises (pure) cognitive elements (which is usually seen as a basic learning mode at a university), practice and professional-bound elements (integration of theory and practice and professional growth and development) as well as self-regulative elements. Based on this, the research also reveals that, when learning, adult learners intend to do it holistically. In phenomenographic parlance the results indicate that when learning the adult learners are to varying degrees simultaneously aware of all those elements (cognition, practise, professional growth and development, self-regulation) presented in the outcome space.

8.2 Contribution to Research and Practice

When evaluating the contribution of the research, two important questions were raised by the present researcher. Firstly, does this research contribute to educational research with regard to adult learners' learning? And secondly, does this research contribute to pedagogical practices in university adult education? Although the questions are posed individually, in fact they are in relation to each other, since contribution to research benefits pedagogical practices and contribution to pedagogical practices, in turn, often poses challenges for further research. The first question above is related to the third research question of the study.

The researcher's own estimation of the contribution of this research is that investigating adult learners' learning experiences using a phenomenographic research approach has been of value. This valuation is also supported by Entwistle (1997a, 130), who notes that phenomenographic qualitative research can offer insights which are likely to have been achieved using another research approach, and which contribute to a better understanding of learning in higher education.

All in all, in the field of the present research (adult learners' degree-oriented university education alongside working-life) there is hardly any of this kind of phenomenographic research, and therefore, by its mere existence, this research contributes to the research field it advocates. Most phenomenographic studies in university settings involve mainstream students (see e.g. Tynjälä 1997, 1999b) but not those whose studies are pursued while in full-time employment.

Furthermore, I have observed that in numerous studies (at least within the national research context) applying phenomenography, it has been used as just a method of analysis but not as a holistic research approach taking into consideration the special premises phenomenography implies. In addition, phenomenography has evolved in recent years but this development towards new phenomenography is in my view not yet generally been sufficiently recognised when conducting phenomenographic research. Hence, it might be reasonable to propose here that both the findings and the method by which they were obtained make fresh contributions to the field. Therefore, with this investigation I hope to have taken a tiny step towards theoretical and methodological improvements with regard to university level adult learners' learning and education. In addition, although the findings of the present research are specific to the phenomenon scrutinised, the phenomenographic research approach used here is not restricted to it.

Moreover, I contend that the findings of this study are of value because they increase, as was also originally intended, the knowledge base of adult learners' learning in general and learners' learning experiences in particular within the context of the research. By finding and establishing the qualitative different variations in how learning is experienced by adult learners, the research offers a concrete foundation for a better grasp of the phenomena relating to adults' learning, and specifically of their experiences of learning at a university. In so doing, the research has a good opportunity to extend pedagogues' and educators' awareness about the distinctive ways of experiencing learning. This in turn, I hope, might result in pedagogical practices of good quality, leading to successful learning. Thus, as it is, the contribution of the research is largely in the hands of its readers and users.

Finally it is my hope that the present research will, at least, initiate a debate relating to a phenomenographic research approach in the education research community. If such a discussion starts up the research at hand will have made a valuable contribution to its research community, and will have been worth doing.

8.3 Implications for Research and Practice

Marton and Booth (1997, 135) characterise phenomenography as a research approach with a strong educational interest. According to them (ibid.) it originates from educational interest and it aspires to serve it as well. Consequently, this phenomenographic research is responsible for disseminating its results to the use of educational research community as well as educational practice. Below, the implications of the research are discussed in terms of implications for research using phenomenography and implications for pedagogical practices.

8.3.1 Implications for Research using Phenomenography

This section aims to answer the question: What implications does this phenomenographic research have for the research community?

I agree with Åkerlind (2005b, 321) in suggesting that phenomenography is often adapted without a clear understanding of the unique methodological requirements of this approach. As has become visible throughout the book, the phenomenographic research approach really has a great deal of unique principles of which the researcher must be aware and which he/she ought to take into consideration while conducting the kind of research. My opinion is that failure on the part of the researcher to make a commitment to a phenomenographic framework may jeopardise the scientific rigour of the research.

As already mentioned in this chapter, phenomenography is as often as not in the field of the present research applied as just a method of analyses and adrift of its basic premises. Therefore, this research has paid particular attention in manifesting what those unique requirements behind phenomenographic approach are and how they holistically guide the research process. That is, however, not to assert that in the present research those requirements are exhaustively understood or adapted. However, it is an admission that underlying the phenomenographic research approach there are ontological and epistemological assumptions, a theoretical basis and methodological requirements and which the present research endeavours to pursue.

All in all, in order to foster scientific rigour this research challenges the researchers dealing with the phenomenographic approach to take seriously into account its underlying assumptions and principles and evolve them to be even more explicit and applicable to research of high quality.

8.3.2 Implications for Pedagogical Practices

This section aims to answer the question: What implications do the findings of the research have for the pedagogical practices of adult learners?

The findings show that there are variations in adult learners' ways of experiencing their learning. Hence, to concur effectively with learners' various ways of experiencing their learning, the pedagogues are challenged to vary in their pedagogical practices. Variation, for instance, in teaching methods may open up learners' opportunities to experience things differently instead of experiencing them perhaps more or less as taken for granted. As Runesson (1999, see also 2006), for instance, argues, excellence in pedagogy has very much to do with what aspects of the object of learning are subjected to variation. The power of variation is also confirmed by Wood (2006, 55), suggesting that for learning to occur, it is necessary for relevant variation to be experienced by the learner.

As became apparent from the outcome space constituted in the research, adult learners experience their learning in a multidimensional way. It is a combination of cognition, practice, professional growth and development as well self-regulation of learning. This multidimensional way of experiencing learning calls for pedagogues and educators to deal with a broader domain of expertise than might so far have been customary or even essential in universities.

Furthermore, the findings of the research challenge the university pedagogues and educators dealing with adult learners to take into account, alongside a purely cognitive dimension, a practical dimension connected to learning. The practical orientation has not so far been common in university education, as this education has taken its point of departure from disciplinary (declarative) knowledge. The findings of the research, however, imply that considering adult learners, whose studies are pursued while in full-time employment, it might be preferable to make use of practice-bound domains alongside disciplinary-bound domains. This viewpoint is also supported by Bromme and Tillema (1995, 266), who take the view that becoming a professional is not a process of merely substituting theory with experience but a process of fusing theory and experience together. Related to this theory-practice dilemma Bromme and Tillema propose professional knowledge as a solution. That knowledge "includes not only special information about the facts and proven methods of problem solving, but also information which is required to define and understand the problems a professional is confronted with" (ibid., 263).

Associated with the previous concern, the findings also call for combining university studies with learners' overall professional growth and development. Cranton et al. (2003, 33) stress that when dealing with the issue of professional development it is important to involve the learner as a whole person. This means that pedagogues and educators need to take into account learners' values, beliefs, and assumptions about their profession and ways of seeing the world.

As the study showed, self-regulation of learning is an essential part of adults' learning. In order to accomplish meaningful learning (as opposed to rote learning), learners are supposed to actively self-regulate their learning processes (van Eekelen et al. 2005, 447). However, it cannot be taken for granted that every adult is capable of deliberately self-regulating his/her learning (see e.g Vermunt 1996, 1998; Oosterheert & Vermunt 2001), and therefore, this matter should be taken into particular consideration throughout the pedagogical practices by pedagogues but also by learners themselves. Ruohotie (2000, 11) points out that learners who, in their own opinion are able to control their learning, are more likely than other learners to use deep information processing approaches. This is the goal of university studies.

Finally, it was a source of surprise that only few learners' ways of experiencing learning were attached to those most sophisticated categories, though the fundamental aim of university studies is to foster learners' high order thinking skills, including metacognition, likewise their growth and development towards expertise in their own domains. On the other hand, the variation in experiencing learning identified in this research does not only result from adult learners' activities in the university; they also extend back into the learners' previous experiences and backgrounds as well as forwards into their everyday contexts of professional activity (e.g. Wood 2006, 64). This shows that the experience derives from "juxtaposing what we see and remember; what we experience now and have experienced before" (Marton et al. 2004, 17).

Summarising the above implications derived from the findings of the research, I conclude that the findings challenge university pedagogues and educators dealing with adult learners, to develop the kind of pedagogical practices which facilitate a genuine combination of theoretical and practical learning as well as learners' self-regulation of learning.

8.4 Recommendations for Further Research

Having considered the contributions and implications of the present research with regard to adult learners' learning in a university setting, some suggestions which may be fruitful areas for further research are presented below.

This research constituted an outcome space which reveals that adult learners' ways of experiencing learning are a combination of cognition, practice, professional growth and self-regulation of learning. However there is without a doubt a need to verify the findings of the small scale qualitative research presented here. Therefore, further research checking the consistency and stability of the findings is needed.

The research findings revealed that there were numerous learners whose ways of experiencing learning were attached to the hierarchically lower categories. This calls for longitudinal investigation as to whether the experiences of learning change or remain more or less stable over time. However, there is no reason to expect an individual to be restricted to a particular way of viewing learning over time (e.g. Åkerlind 1999, 11). On the contrary, there is evidence that the ways of experiencing can change. For example, Eklund-Myrskog (1997) and Tynjälä

(1999) found in their studies that the ways of experiencing learning developed and became more complex over a period of time.

It would also be noteworthy to find out how the different ways of experiencing learning found in this research are related to adult learners' actual learning outcomes, both as students and as professionals. Are those learners whose learning experiences were attached to the most sophisticate ways of experiencing learning also successful as learners, when assessed, for instance, by means of grades awarded? And is the converse true? Furthermore, how do the varying degrees in ways of experiencing learning reflect to one's professional activity and impact further on his/her work community in the form, for instance, of organisational development?

Further fruitful research questions include how pedagogues and educators of adult learners experience learning. What is the relation between learners' and pedagogues' experiences of learning? Are there similarities or differences between learners and pedagogues' ways of experiencing learning? And how do they affect high quality learning outcomes.

And finally, I would hope to see more phenomenographic research, not just using phenomenography as a method of analyses, as is frequently the case, but rather as a holistic research approach, in which despite the complexities the researcher adheres to the principles behind the phenomenographic research approach, as the present research aimed at to do.

9 EVALUATION OF THE RESEARCH

One of the aims of science is to build up valid knowledge of reality (see e.g. Moilanen 2000, 378; Puolimatka 2002b, 466). For that reason the next sections evaluate the validity and reliability of the present research. Particular emphasis is placed on how validity and reliability are adapted to ensure the truthfulness (truth value) of this phenomenographic research. According to Sandberg (2005, 58) the principal question of validity in this type of research is how the researcher can justify that his/her interpretations are truthful to participants' lived experience within the theoretical and methodological perspectives taken. The principal question of reliability concerns the procedure for achieving these truthful interpretations. (ibid.)

In addition to the evaluation of validity and reliability also the generalisation (transferability) of the findings and the ethics of the research are scrutinised here. As the gathering procedures and the data obtained for the research was already evaluated in Section 6.3, the discussion below concentrates mainly on validating the results (categorisation) and knowledge claims constituted via interpretive analysis of that data.

When establishing knowledge about some phenomenon of reality, every research approach makes specific assumptions about the nature of the reality under investigation (ontology) and about the nature of knowledge (epistemology) (Sandberg 2005, 47). Associated with that, Giorgi (2002, 2) enumerates three factors the researcher should take into account when evaluating qualitative research. These factors are the philosophy of science within which one works, the discipline to which one belongs, and the subfield of specialization that one pursues. This research works within the phenomenological philosophy of science and belongs to the discipline of education. The specialization pursued here is the phenomenographical research approach which stipulates that knowledge is constituted through lived experience and making sense of reality. Therefore knowledge is here strongly correlated with subjectivity. As stated by Giorgi (2002, 9), "Perhaps there are things or events-in-themselves, but there is no knowledge-in-itself. There is only knowledge for a human subject who apprehends it." The criteria of the present research need to be scrutinised in accordance with the stipulations above.

9.1 Theories of Truth

The issue of what is valid knowledge involves the philosophical question of truth (e.g. Kvale 1989, 75; 1996, 238). The four classical theories of truth are correspondence, coherence, pragmatic and consensus (see e.g. Puolimatka 2002b). In short, the correspondence theory of truth concerns whether the knowledge claim corresponds to the objective world. The coherence theory refers to the consistency and internal logic of a knowledge claim. Pragmatic theory relates the truth to practical consequences. (Kvale 1989, 75.) Consensus theory of truth stresses the importance of the research community in the verification of interpretations (Moilanen 2000, 388).

Based on the fact that in an interpretative study, like this phenomenographic research, the researcher makes subjective interpretations of subjective interpretations, Moilanen (2000, 378) has posed an essential question "Is there any place for the notion of true"? Uljens (1996, 115) asks likewise "How does then a non-dualist answer why one theory is false and another true?" It is, however, argued here, referring to Sandberg (2005, 47), that although objective truth cannot be achieved, truth claims are feasible using criteria consistent with the basic assumptions underlying a phenomenographic research approach.

Moilanen (2000) as well as Puolimatka (2002b) noted that the correspondence theory of truth is often considered unsuitable for qualitative research. Moilanen (2000, 377) supposes the reason for that elimination to be that there is no way to match interpretations and reality because reality itself consists of changing interpretations. This also entails that it is impossible to reach absolute truth about some phenomenon (in principle) since we ourselves continuously make new interpretations. And therefore, scientific truth is, according to this position, absolute only in a relative sense. (Uljens 1996, 112-113.) This means here that the truth, achieved within interpretive approaches, will not be final and unambiguous but is rather an ongoing and open process of knowledge claims correcting each other (Sandberg 2005, 52). Comprehending knowledge and truth here as relative to ontological and epistemological assumptions surmounts the problem of extreme relativism that may arise from the interpretive rejection of objective truth claims (e.g. ibid., 47). But, in spite of all, one aim of science is to make correct knowledge claims in interpretations of reality and this aim makes the correspondence theory of truth useful (Moilanen 2000, 388) in this research.

Therefore, as far as the correspondence theory is concerned, a phenomenographic researcher does not ask how well his/her research findings correspond to the phenomenon as it exists in reality, but instead, how well his/her findings correspond to human experience of that phenomenon. And consequently, a phenomenographer does not relate his/her knowledge claims to reality as such but to one's experience of the reality. This is because, according to non-dualist ontology, there is no distinction between experience and reality (experience is an internal relationship between subject and object, and in that sense experience is reality) (Uljens 1996, 115). Associated with this, Uljens (1996, 115-116, see also Puolimatka 2002b) claims that in phenomenographic research the researcher should talk about correspondence to experience and forget correspondence to reality.

Sandberg's (2005) suggestion of truth as intentional fulfilment, includes the same idea as that discussed above. There truth "can be achieved when the researcher's interpretation allows the research object to appear on its own conditions within the perspective taken" (ibid., 52). Larsson (1998, 18-19) also avoids using the concept of correspondence and instead, with the same idea, chooses to talk about the empirical anchorage of knowledge claims. In that way it is not one-to-one relation but a relation between interpretation and its claim to be grounded in the empirical world.

In this research the question of truth is seen similarly as in Jokinen and Juhila (1991, 66). This means that, even though correspondence theory is not be used (in objective sense) and the research does not aim to produce the real image of reality, the interpretation must correspond to the data (participants' lived experience). It is not about whether the interpretation is true or untrue, but whether it is possible and credible in relation to the data. This means that the correspondence theory of truth is detectable here.

9.1.1 Validity of the Research

The most common definition of validity is epitomised by the question: are we measuring what we think we are measuring (Kerlinger 1973, 457)? Two types of validity criteria, named communicative and pragmatic validity by Kvale (1989, 1995, 1996), are commonly used within phenomenographic research (Åkerlind 2005a, 330). In addition to those criteria Sandberg (2005, 54 referring to Lather 1993, 1995 and Richardson 1995) has recently proposed a criterion termed transgressive validity. In short, whereas communicative validity makes it possible to check the coherence of the interpretation, pragmatic validity also pays attention to the applicability of knowledge claims. And finally, transgressive validity aims to help the researcher to become aware of his/her possible taken-for-granted frameworks. (Sandberg 2005, 56-58.)

All those three above-mentioned criteria of validity were applied in this research to strive in an endeavour to justify the knowledge claims as true (ensuring validity of the findings). In the following their application will be discussed in detail in the same order as they were introduced above.

Communicative Validity

Marton (1997, 100) stipulates that "...once the outcome space of a phenomenon has been revealed, it should be communicated in such a way that other researchers could recognise instances of the different ways of experiencing the phenomenon in question." Here Marton is referring to communicative validity. In practice communicative validity involves testing the validity of knowledge claims in a dialogue (Kvale 1995). According to Sandberg (2005, 55), this means discussing the findings with other researchers and professionals in the practice being investigated. Although the original researcher is the main producer of knowledge claims, it is ultimately an intersubjective judgment that determines whether the original researcher's knowledge claim is true. This is so because, "by discussing with different communities of interpreters, knowledge claims can be refined or challenged as limited." (ibid., 56.) In this research communicative validity was sought by presenting evolving and final findings (outcome space) several times in postgraduates research seminars, through discussions with supervisors and other researchers as well as with postgraduate students engaged in phenomenographic research. In those discussions I gained valuable insight, which challenged the established knowledge claims.

Sometimes communicative validity is also implemented as participants' validation (member checking). Here the validity procedure shifts from the researcher to participants in the research (see e.g. Creswell & Miller 2000, 127). However, seeking direct feedback from the participants was not used in this study. The reason was that the interpretations were made on a collective basis and were based on the interviews as a holistic group, not individual interviews. Associated with that, the categorisation was established across individuals and hence there were no anticipation that a single participant would identify the categorisation. As Kelly (2002, 7) asks "With each individual recognising only some elements of each system, how can they validate the system?" However, the preliminary results of the research were twice presented in seminars attended by numerous TUKEVA students, including several of those who took part in the present research. In addition to these, the seminars were attended by TUKEVA students' educators and employers as well as representatives from the National Board of Education in Finland. The presentations in those seminars and the feedback I received there are assumed to have strengthened the communicative validity of the research.

Still considering communicative validity in phenomenographic research, it also includes the researcher providing her report with adequate quotes to demonstrate to the reader the structure and meaning of the categories of, and the processes through which the categories have been constituted (e.g. Entwistle, 1997a). The results of this research are presented so that the knowledge claims are connected to the empirical evidence in the form of adequate quotes from the data. The process through which I constituted the categories has been thoroughly and comprehensively communicated via different stages of analysis.

Achieving high communicative validity calls for coherency and consistency of knowledge claims. The present research strove for coherency and consistency of knowledge claims by applying a kind of hermeneutic circle when analysing and interpreting the data. Hermeneutic circle means (Larsson 1998, 22) that an interpretation is built up by the interplay between part and whole. In practice it meant that at the beginning of the interpretation of the data my understanding was based on a general picture I had created by means of what I knew so far as a result of interviewing and reading transcripts. The more I read the transcripts, the more details I learnt; these I understood in the light of the interpretation I had so far created. I also changed my interpretations of the phenomenon because of new details that were revealed to me. The interpretation therefore assumed interplay between parts and whole.

In addition, the results of the research are in accordance with the recommendations of Marton and Booth (1997, 125), who explain that in phenomenographic research the criterion for the validity and truthfulness of each category of description is that they stand in a clear relationship with the phenomenon of investigation and also have a logical relationship with one another. This research has been implemented in accordance with the tenets of phenomenographic research and there are clear and logical relations between each of the identified ways of experiencing learning. Those relationships are captured in the outcome space (see Figure 6)

Pragmatic Validity

By pragmatic validation of a knowledge claim justification is superseded by application and it represents a stronger knowledge claim than a mere agreement through dialogue (Kvale 1995). Hence, pragmatic validity can compensate a weakness in communicative validity (Sandberg 2005, 56). Entwistle (1997a, 129) refers to pragmatic validity by stating: "For researchers in higher education, however, the test is generally not its [phenomenography's] theoretical purity, but its value in producing useful insights into teaching and learning." As discussed in the first chapter of the book, the purpose of my research endeavour was to arrive at deeper understanding of the core element of education, that of learning. I assume that understanding students' ways of experiencing learning provides a good basis for improving teaching and learning. Gaining insight into learning this research should therefore enrich pedagogy and contribute to research on learning. Since the pragmatic criterion refers to the usefulness of the findings, these ideas are dealt with as contributions and implications of the research in Chapter 7.

Transgressive Validity

Sandberg (2005, 57) states that the communicative and pragmatic criteria of validity tend to encourage the researcher to search chiefly for consistent and unequivocal interpretations of participant's lived experience. Due to this there may be a danger that these criteria of validity cause the researcher to ignore possible contradictions in the data of lived experience investigated. Sandberg recommends correcting this weakness by transgressive validity. Transgressive validity should help the researcher to pay more attention to irresolvable contradictions and tensions. However, its prime aim is to make the researcher aware of taken-for-granted frameworks. (ibid., 57-58).

To strive for transgressive validity during the analyses, I deliberately from time to time I searched for contradictions rather than for coherence in the data as well as in the evolving category system.

To sum up, communicated, pragmatic, and transgressive validity criteria were used to generate valid knowledge in this research. These various criteria were not seen to contradict each other but rather to compensate each other's weaknesses (e.g. Sandberg 2005). Communicative validity was used to achieve coherence between my interpretations and the empirical material investigated. Pragmatic validity entailed ensuring the usefulness of the findings. And finally, as suggested by Sandberg (2005), the weaknesses in communicative and pragmatic validity for not paying enough attention to possible contradictions in the data, were here compensated by applying transgressive validity.

9.1.2 Reliability of the Research

Reliability in phenomenographic research is not considered by Cope (2004, 9) to have the same sense as reliability in qualitative research in general. More specifically, in general it refers to the replicability of results, which means "... if another researcher repeated the research project...would arrive at the same results" (Booth 1992, 64). From the perspective of phenomenographic research, that idea would assume a replicability of the outcome space; that another researcher when furnished with the same empirical material would create exactly the same outcome space as the original researcher. Regarding replicability in phenomenographic research there is, however, in the literature, a consensus that it is not a reasonable question to ask at all. (Cope 2004, 9.) Cope (ibid. referring to Burns 1994) clarifies why this idea of replicability is not in accordance with phenomenographical principles. In keeping with those principles, human beings experience phenomena in the world in different ways. Why then should different researchers not experience the variation in participants lived experience in different ways? In sum, replicability is neither consistent with the relational nature of the constitution of categories nor the dynamic nature of awareness (e.g. McKenzie 2003, 92).

Marton (1997, 100), as well, takes the view that the demand for replicability is neither justified nor desirable. This is because he considers phenomenographic analysis to be a process of discovery: "Finding out the different ways in which a phenomenon can be experienced is as much a discovery as the finding of some new plants on a distant island. The discovery does not have to be replicable..." (ibid.) However, it is suggested by Marton that as far as such a judgement of results is concerned there should be a reasonable degree of agreement between two independent and competent researchers. (ibid.) The idea behind Marton's suggestion is that in order to detect the bias and to evaluate the quality of research there is a need for other evaluators besides the researcher him/herself. (see e.g. Moilanen 2000, 384.)

Interjudge (co-judge) procedure is often used in phenomenographic research to evaluate the category systems developed (Sandberg 1997, 206). The use of interjudge reliability in phenomenographic research has been described by Säljö (1988, 45) as measuring "the communicability of categories and thus gives the researcher information that someone else can see the same differences in the material as he or she has done."

An interjudge reliability procedure was also used in this research as an indicator of a reliable correspondence between data and the results. The co-judge was an undergraduate in education, working as a research assistant in the Research Centre for Vocational Education. She was familiar with the phenomenographic research approach and with the broader TUKEVA research project, but she did not know the empirical material of the present research. The co-judge was informed about the proposed structure of subcategories (in total 21 subcategories) and the criterion attributes for each category were made explicit to her in written form. She was also given all the same quotations (in total 512) in alphabetical order according to the first letter of the sentence that the researcher had used in constituting the categories. It is important to note here that the co-judge did not have access to the complete transcripts, but only the quotations (pool of meanings) which were extracted from the transcripts. The co-judge was then asked to place each quotation in the subcategories she deemed most suitable. If the co-judge found quotations that did not fit into any category, she was asked to create a new category or let those quotations under our mutual discussion. The co-judge was not therefore obliged to follow the categorisation created by me but was given an opportunity to make her own interpretations and to create new categories as she deemed it necessary. The co-judge procedure was implemented using the same qualitative data processing software program NVivo 6.1. as I used. The interjudge procedure took approximately three months.

Interjudge reliability of categories of description can be claimed on the basis of the percentage agreement between the researchers' classifications. According to Marton (1997, 100) there needs to be a "reasonable degree of agreement," which means that two researchers agree in at least two-thirds of the cases, whereas Säljö (1988) believes an agreement of 80 to 90 % is appropriate. The degree of intersubjective agreement at the level of subcategories in this research was around 90 %. Thus, there was total agreement in 465 out of the 512 cases. No new categories were established by the co-judge, but some propositions, which were submitted for further elaboration, were made. In 47 of the remaining cases agreement was reached after discussion. This kind of discussion is called a dialogic reliability check (Åkerlind 2005a, 331). In a dialogic reliability check agreement between researchers is reached through discussion and, criticism of the data and each researcher's interpretive hypotheses (ibid.).

The use of interjudge reliability in phenomenographic studies has been criticised by Sandberg (1997; 2005). He argues that interjudge reliability is inconsistent with the relational character of phenomenographic research. As an alternative to it, Sandberg advocates the procedure he calls interpretive awareness. Interpretive awareness means "to acknowledge and explicitly deal with our subjectivity throughout the research process instead of overlooking it" (Sandberg 2005, 59). In practice interpretive awareness entails demonstrating that a researcher's interpretations during the data analysis have been controlled and checked (Cope 2004, 14). In this research interpretive awareness was implemented in the form of epoché, which has already been discussed in connection with interviewing, in Section 6.2.1.

In addition to interjudge reliability and interpretive awareness triangulation was also applied to ensure the reliability of the research. Triangulation is (e.g. Creswell & Miller 2000; Larsson 1998) originally a maritime term which means that it is possible to estimate one's position by noting the grades on the compass to several points in the terrain. Using triangulation a researcher searches for convergence among multiple and different sources of knowledge to form categories in the research (Creswell & Miller 2000, 126) and congruence between different sources is a sign of validity (Larsson 1998, 20). In this research triangulation was implemented by providing corroborating evidence collected through two different methods, that is, through interviewing (spoken data) and through written accounts. Interview data was used as primary data and written accounts as supplementary data to ensure the reliability and validity of the research. Both data sets were analysed in the same manner but in independent processes. The variation between these two sources was identical, denoting that the same kind of categorisation could be established for both data sources.

Table 14 summarises the evaluation of the validity and reliability of the research.

Table 14. *Summary of the evaluation of validity and reliability of the research*

	Criteria	Practices used to satisfy the criteria
Validity	**Communicative validity** - involves testing validity of knowledge claims in a dialogue	I presented the findings; i.e. variations in the ways of experiencing learning and the categorisation several times to and discussed within the research community. The findings were also subjected to discourse with the members of TUKEVA's varying interest groups.
		I have presented the findings of the study in this report so that the knowledge claims are connected to the empirical evidence in the form of adequate quotes from the data.
		The report includes full and open accounts of the methods and results of the study.
	- involves testing validity of knowledge claims via coherency and consistency	I made the interpretations by means of a hermeneutic circle; i.e., the interpretations were constituted in an iterative manner by a successive circular relation between the parts and the whole.
	Pragmatic validity - involves testing validity of knowledge claims by application	The study aimed at gaining useful knowledge and understanding of adult learners' learning in a university setting. It also strove to contribute to basic research on the learning of adults and methods exploring that learning.
		Since the pragmatic criterion refers to the usefulness of findings, these matters are addressed here as contributions and implications of the study (see Section 8.2 & 8.3).
	Transgressive validity - involves testing validity of knowledge claims by paying attention to possible contradictions in interpretations	I deliberately searched from time to time for contradictions rather than for coherence in the data and in the evolving categorisation in order to avoid possible preconceptions.
Reliability	**Interpretive awareness** - reliability is checked through researcher's acknowledging his/her subjectivity	Interpretive awareness was implemented throughout the study process in the form of epoché; i.e. I tried to suppress my prior knowledge and experiences of the learning of adults and check that the interpretations made were based on participants' learning experiences instead of my own.
		My background was openly acknowledged to the reader.
	Triangulation - reliability is checked through searching for convergence among multiple and different sources of knowledge	Triangulation was adapted by providing corroborating evidence collected through two different methods; i.e. interviewing (spoken data) and written accounts.
	Interjudge reliability - reliability is checked through a reasonable degree of agreement between two independent researchers	The study made use of a co-judge procedure. The co-judge was informed about the proposed structure of the categories and the criterion attributes for each category. She was then given the quotations extracted from the transcripts, and asked to place each one of them into the categories she preferred the most suitable. Intersubjective agreement was around 90 %.

Dialogic reliability check - reliability is checked through discussion and criticism by independent researchers	Those quotations not placed into any categories by the co-judge, were submitted to further elaboration. Agreement was reached in negotiation between me and the co-judge.

9.2 Generalisation of the Research

In qualitative research, the aim with respect to external validity (external validity asks in what contexts the findings can be applied) is to ascertain whether or not the results can be applied in other settings (Malterud 2001, 484). From the perspective of phenomenographic research the question concerns if the findings can be generalised to other situations at the individual level, or to a population, or to other populations, at the group of people (Marton & Booth 1997, 127). Accordingly, generalisation (transferability) would in this research mean: Do the findings and knowledge claims of this research only relate to the students who participated in the research or only TUKEVA students, or can they also be regarded as applicable in similar kinds of education on a more general level?

Phenomenographic research makes knowledge claims about the ways in which some phenomenon (here learning) in the world is experienced by a particular group of individuals (here purposefully sampled TUKEVA students) in relation to a certain context (here to university studies). As Åkerlind (2005a, 323) states "ideally, the outcomes (results) represent the full range of possible ways of experiencing the phenomenon in question, at this particular point in time for the population represented by the sample group collectively." Moreover, it should be noted here that phenomenography is founded on the relational view of knowledge, in which knowledge is neither absolute nor objective nor subjective, but it is based on a certain type of encounter, that is, being in relation with reality. Therefore, in a strict sense, knowledge is valid or invalid only within that certain encounter and inside a certain setting into a relation, and its validity cannot necessarily be generalised to concern other kinds of relations. (e.g. Karvonen 1997.) The previous idea also concurs with Rauhala's (e.g. 1989; 1992) situationality.

However, the aim of research is to produce knowledge that can be disseminated and applied beyond the original research setting (e.g. Malterud 2001, 484). Congruent with that, Marton and Booth (1997, 128), argue that even if the delivery of different ways of experiencing the phenomenon in question may not straightforwardly be generalised to any population, the researcher can still claim to have identified the variation in how the phenomenon in question might be experienced by certain kind of group of people. Moreover, even if the empirical statements concerning those people cannot be generalised, the variation itself might very well turn out to be so. (ibid.)

This research was conducted in a formal educational university setting with regard to adult education, and it is supposed here that despite the limitations discussed above, the findings of the research are applicable and useful in similar settings but not to population groups at large in various educational contexts. Hence, in order give the reader an opportunity to ascertain for which context the findings might especially provide valuable knowledge I have made the philosophical, theoretical and methodological underpinnings of the research transparent. Furthermore, the context of the research and characteristics of participants involved as well as the methods used are presented in a manner that the user of this research can make his/her own estimations about the applicability of the findings to other contexts.

9.3   Ethics of the Research

When doing research, a human sciences researcher is recommended to take guidance from the ethical principles on research with human participants (e.g. Moustakas 1994, 110). Especially in the personal lived experience method, which this research advocates, the relationship between researcher and participant is emphasised as ethically crucial. Because the researcher enters this relationship with his/her own special intentions and purposes, care and responsibility should be taken towards participants, i.e how the researching affects them. When a researcher enters into a relationship with participants, and asks them to share their experiences, there is always a possibility, for instance, of unethically construing their lived, told and relived accounts of experiences according to researcher's own intentions and purposes. (e.g. Clandinin & Connelly 1994, 422.)

Furthermore, as the researcher moves from field texts (here interviews) to research texts (here from the interviews to the transcripts and to the final report), the ethical issues continue to be of great value. That is, lived experience method involves authentic human beings and, not just texts. Hence, the researcher should pay attention to the after-effects the research may possibly cause for the participants involved. (e.g. Clandinin & Connelly 1994, 422.)

It is suggested that the research reported here maintained good ethical standards, particularly when entering into a relationship with the participants, handling their accounts of lived experience and avoiding negative after-effects. Some of the ethical principles employed in this research are summarised below but they are mainly discussed throughout the research in connection with their original location.

In the beginning of data gathering participants' willingness to participate in the research was ascertained by the researcher. I then provided the participants with detailed information regarding the nature and purpose of the research they were attending. Their role in the research and contribution to it was also outlined. The data gathered through interviews and written accounts were not used in the research without participant's consent. Furthermore, information that I considered confidential was removed from the data to protect the identity and to ensure the anonymity of the participant. In addition, to ensure complete anonymity, I included no names or codes of the participants in the quotes. The participants were moreover free to withdraw from the research at any time.

REFERENCES

Achtenhagen, F. (1995). Commentary. Fusing experience and theory – socio-political and cognitive issues. *Learning and Instruction* 5, 409-417.
Adawi, T., Berglund, A., Booth, S. & Ingerman, Å. (2002). *On context in phenomenographic research on understanding heat and temperature.* Revised paper presented at EARLI 2001. Fribourg, Switzerland.
Alvesson, M. (2003). Beyond neopositivists, romantics and localists: A reflexive approach to interviews in organizational research. *Academy of Management Review* 28, 1-13.
Anderberg, E. (2000). *Language meaning and understanding. A phenomenographic perspective.* Paper presented at the Workshop on Updating Phenomenography. May 2000. Hong Kong.
Anfara,V. & Brown, K. (2001). *Qualitative analysis on stage: Making the research project more public.* Paper presented at the Annual Meeting of the AERA. April 2001. Seatle, WA.
Arvidson, P.S. (2003). A lexicon of attention: From cognitive science to phenomenology. *Phenomenology and the Cognitive Sciences* 2, 99-132.
Ashworth, P. & Lucas, U. (1998). What is the "world" of phenomenography? *Scandinavian Journal of Educational Research* 42 (4), 415-431.
Ashworth, P. & Lucas, U. (2000). Achieving empathy and engagement: a practical approach to the design, conduct and reporting of phenomenographic research. *Studies in Higher Education* 25 (3), 295-308.
Bandura, A. (1977). Self-efficacy: Toward a unifying theory of behavioural change. *Psychological Review 84* (2), 191-215.
Bandura, A. (Ed.) (1995). *Self-efficacy in changing societies.* New York: Cambridge University Press.
Bandura, A. (1997). *Self-efficacy: The exercise of control.* New York: W.H. Freeman and Company.
Bandura, A. (in press). Towards a psychology of human agency. *Perspectives on Psychological Science.*
Barnard, A., McCosker, H. & Gerber, R. (1999). Phenomenography: a qualitative research approach for exploring understanding in health care. *Qualitative Health Research* 9 (2), 212-226.
Beairsto, B. (1996). Professional growth and development: What is it and how do we know if it is working? In P. Ruohotie & P. Grimmett (Eds.) *Professional growth and development. Direction, delivery and dilemmas.* University of Tampere and Simon Fraser University, 91-111.
Beairsto, B. & Ruohotie, P. (2003). Empowering professionals as lifelong learners. In B. Beairsto, M. Klein & P. Ruohotie (Eds.) *Professional learning and leadership.* Hämeenlinna: Research Centre for Vocational Education, University of Tampere, 115-145.
Beaty, E., G. Dall'Alba & F. Marton (1990). *Conceptions of academic learning.* Occasional paper 90.4, RMIT, Educational Research and Development Unit, Victoria University of Technology, Melbourne.

Berglund, A. (2005). *Learning computer systems in a distributed project course: The what, why, how and where*. Uppsala Dissertations from the Faculty of Science and Technology, 62. Acta Universitatis Upsaliensis.

Biggs, J. (1999). *Teaching for quality learning at university*. Buckingham, U.K: Open University Press.

Biggs, J. (2003). *Teaching for quality learning at university. What the student does*. Buckingham, U.K: SRHE and Open University Press.

Blumer, H. (1969). *Symbolic interactionism: Perspective and method*. Englewood Cliffs, NJ: Prentice Hall.

Boekaerts, M. (1997). Self-regulated learning: A new concept embraced by researchers, policy makers, educators, teachers, and students. *Learning and Instruction* 7 (2), 161-186.

Boekaerts, M., Pintrich, P.R., & Zeidner, M. (Eds.) (2000). *Handbook of self-regulation*. San Diego, CA:Academic Press.

Booth, S. (1992). *Learning to program: A phenomenographic perspective*. Göteborg Studies in Educational Sciences 89. Acta Universitatis Gothoburgensis.

Booth, S. (2001). Learning computer science and engineering in context. *Computer science education* 11 (3), 169-188.

Booth, S. (2004). Engineering education and the pedagogy of awareness. In C. Baillie & I. Moore (Eds.) *Effective learning and teaching in engineering*. London: Kogan Page, 9-23.

Booth, S. & Hulte'n, M. (2003). Opening dimensions of variation: An empirical study of learning in a web-based discussion. *Instructional Science* 31, 65-86.

Bouffard, T., Boisvert, J., Vezeau, C. & Larouche, C. (1995). The impact of goal orientation on self-regulation and performance among college students. *The British Journal of Educational Psychology* 65, 317-329.

Boulton-Lewis, G.M., Marton, F., Lewis, D.C. & Wills, L.A. (2000). Learning in formal and informal context: conceptions and strategies of Aboriginal and Torres Strait Islanders university students. *Learning and Instruction* 10 (5), 393-414.

Boulton-Lewis, G.M. & Wilss, L.A. (2004). Maximising data use: Mixed qualitative methods. Paper presented at the meeting of the EARLY-SIG 17. October 2004. Freudenstadt-Lauterbad, Germany.

Boulton-Lewis, G.M., Wilss, L.A. & Lewis, D. C. (2001). Changes in conceptions of learning for indigenous Australian university students. *British Journal of Educational Psychology* 71, 327-341.

Bowden, J.A. (2000). The nature of phenomenographic research. In J.A. Bowden and E. Walsh (Eds.) Phenomenography. Melbourne: RMIT University Press. <http://informit.com.au/library/print.asp?i=1054>. Accessed 18th March 2004.

Bowden, J.A. (2004). Capabilities-driven curriculum design. In C Baillie & I Moore (Eds) Effective Teaching and Learning in Engineering. London: Kogan Page, 36-47.

Bowden, J.A. & Marton, F. (2004). *The university of learning: Beyond quality and competence in higher education* (paperback ed.). London: RoutledgeFalmer.

Brentano, F. (1973). *Psychology from an empirical standpoint*. London: RoutledgeFalmer and Kegan Paul.

Brentano, F. (1995). *Psychology from an empirical standpoint*. Translated by A. C. Rancurello, D. B. Terrel & L. L. McAlister. London: RoutledgeFalmer.

Bromme, R. & Tillema, H.H. (1995). Introduction. *Learning and Instruction* 5, 261-267.

Bron, A. (2005). Paradigm change in adult education research. In A. Heikkinen (Ed.) *Aikuiskasvatuksen tutkimuspolut*. Helsinki: Kansanvalistusseura, 18-34.

Bruce, C.S. (1992). Teaching end user remote online searching. *Australian Academic and Research Libraries* 23 (1), 11-19.
Bruce, C.S. (1997). *The seven faces of information literacy*. Adelaide: Auslib Press.
Burnett, P.C., Pillay, H., Dart, B.C. (2003). The influences of conceptions of learning and learner self-concept on high school students' approaches to learning, *School Psychology International* 24 (1), 54-66.
Burns, J. (1994). Extending critique within phenomenography. In R. Ballantyne & C. Bruce (Eds.) *Proceedings of phenomenography: Philosophy and practice*. Brisbane, Queensland: QUT Publications and Printing, 71-76.
Case, J.M. (2000). *Students' perceptions of context, approaches to learning and metacognitive development in a second year chemical engineering course*. PhD. thesis, Monash University, Melbourne, Australia.
Charmaz, K. (2000). Constructivist and objectivist methods. In N.K. Denzin & Y.S. Lincoln (Eds.) *Handbook of qualitative research*. (2nd ed.). Thousand Oaks, CA: Sage, 509-535.
Charmaz, K. (2004). Grounded theory: Methodology and theory construction. In N.J. Smelser & P.B. Baltes (Eds.) *International encyclopedia of the social & behavioural sciences*. ScienceDirect online, 6396-6399.
Charmaz, K. (2005). Grounded theory in the 21st century: Applications for advancing social justice studies. In N.K. Denzin & Y.S. Lincoln (Eds.) *The SAGE Handbook of qualitative research* (3rd ed.). Thousand Oaks, CA: Sage, 507-535.
Cherry, N. (1998). Personal communications. In Dunkin, R. (2000). *Using phenomenography to study organisational change*. In J.A. Bowden and E. Walsh (Eds.) Phenomenography. Melbourne: RMIT University Press. <http://informit.com.au/library/print.asp?i=1054>. Accessed 18th March 2004.

Chi, M.T.H. (1992). Conceptual change within and across ontological categories: Examples from learning and discovery in science. In R. Giere (Ed.) *Cognitive models of science: Minnesota studies in the philosophy of science*. Minneapolis, MN: University of Minnesota Press, 129-186.
Chi, M.T.H., Slotta, J.D. & Leeuw, N. (1994). From things to processes: A theory of conceptual change for learning science concept. *Learning and Instruction* 4, 27-43.
Clandinin, D.F. & Connelly, F.M. (1994). Personal Experience Method. In N.K. Denzin & Y.S. Lincoln (Eds.) *Handbook of Qualitative Research*. Thousand Oaks, CA: Sage, 413-427.
Cope, C. (2000). *Educationally critical aspects of the experience of learning about the concept of an information system*. Doctoral thesis. La Trobe University, Bundoora, Australia. <http://ironbark.bendigo.latrobe.edu.au/~cope/cope-thesis.pdf>. Accessed 15th February 2004.
Cope, C. (2004). Ensuring validity and reliability in phenomenographic research using the analytical framework of a structure of awareness. *Qualitative Research Journal* 4 (2), 5-18.
Corno, L. (1993). The best-laid plans. Modern conception of volition and educational research. *Educational Researcher* 22 (2), 14-22.
Corno, L. (1994). Student volition and education: Outcomes, influences, and practices. In B. Zimmerman & D. Schunk (Eds.) *Self-regulation of learning and performance*. Hillsdale, NJ: Lawrence Erlbaum Associates, 229-254.
Cornu, AL. (2005). Building on Jarvis: Towards holistic model of the processes of experimental learning. *Studies in Education of Adults* 37 (2), 166-181.
Cranton, P. & King, K.P. (2003). Transformative learning as a professional development goal. *New Directions for Adult and Continuing Education* 98, 31-37.

Creswell, J.W. & Miller D.L. (2000). Determining validity in qualitative inquiry. *Theory into Practice* 39 (3), 124-131.

Dahlgren, L.O. (1975). *Qualitative differences in learning as a function of content-oriented guidance.* Göteborg: Acta Universitatis Gothoburgensis.

Dahlgren, L.O. (1997). Learning conceptions and outcomes. In F. Marton, D. Hounsell & N. Entwistle (Eds.) *The Experience of Learning.* Edinburgh: Scottish Academic Press, 23-38.

Dahlin, B. & Regmi, M.P. (1997). Conceptions of learning among Nepalese students. *Higher Education* 33, 471–493.

Dennett, D.C. (1997). *Miten mieli toimii?* Suomentanut L. Nivala. Porvoo: WSOY.

Denzin, N.K. & Lincoln, Y.S. (2005). Preface. In N.K. Denzin & Y.S. Lincoln (Eds.) *The SAGE Handbook of qualitative research* (3rd ed.). Thousand Oaks, CA: Sage, ix-xix.

Dewey, J. (1963). *Experience & education.* New York: Collier Books.

Dortins, E. (2002). Reflections on phenomenographic process: interview, transcription and analysis. In A. Goody, J. Herrington & M. Northcote (Eds.) *Proceedings of the 2002 Annual International Conference of the Higher Education Research and Development Society of Australasia (HERDSA), Perth, Australia.* <http://www.herdsa.org.au/publications/>. Accessed at 15th July 2004, 207-213.

Dunkin, R. (2000). *Using phenomenography to study organisational change.* In J.A. Bowden and E. Walsh (Eds.) Phenomenography. Melbourne: RMIT University Press. http://www.informit.com.au/library/samples/PHENOMENOGRAPHY_ERIN/chap_09....>. Accessed 18th May 2004.

Eklund-Myrskog, G. (1998). Students' conceptions of learning in different educational contexts. *Higher Education* 35, 299–316.

Entwistle, N. (1997). Introduction: Phenomenography in higher education. *Higher Education Research & Development* 16 (2), 127-134.

Entwistle, A & Entwistle, N.J. (1992). Experiences of understanding in revising for degree examinations. *Learning and Instruction* 2, 1-22.

Entwistle, NJ. & Entwistle, A. (1991). Contrasting forms of understanding for degree examination the student experience and its implications. *Higher Education* 22, 205-207.

Entwistle, N.J. & Entwistle, D. (2003). Preparing for examinations: the interplay of memorising and understanding, and the development of knowledge objects. *Higher Education Research & Development* 22, (1), 19-41.

Entwistle, N.J. & Ramsden, P. (1983). *Understanding student learning.* London: Groom Helm.

Fazey, J.A. & Marton, F. (2002). Understanding the space of experiential variation. *Active Learning in Higher Education* 3 (3), 234-250.

Francis, H. (1993). Advancing phenomenography: questions of method. *Nordisk Pedagogik* 13 (2), 68-75.

Francis, H. (1996). Advancing phenomenography – questions of method. In G. Dall'Alba & B. Hasselgren (Eds.) *Reflections on Phenomenography. Toward a Methodology?* Göteborg Studies in Educational Sciences 109, Acta Universitatis Gothoburgensis, 35-47.

Franke, A. & Dahlgren, L.O. (1996). Conceptions of mentoring: An empirical study of conceptions of mentoring during the school-based teacher education. *Teaching and Teacher Education* 12 (6), 627-641.

Fraser, D. (2002) *QSR NVivo NUD*IST* Vivo. Reference Guide.* Melbourne, Australia: QSR International Pty.Ltd.

Garcia, T. (1995). The role of motivational strategies in self-regulated learning. In P.R. Pintrich (Ed.) *Understanding self-regulated learning.* San Francisco: Jossey-Bass Publishers, 29-42.

Giorgi, A. (1986). *A phenomenological analysis of descriptions of conceptions of learning obtained from a phenomenographic perspective*. Publications from the Department of Education, Göteborg University. <http://www.ped.gu.se/biorn/phgraph/misc/constr/giorgi.html>. Accessed 13th February 2004.

Giorgi, A. (1990). Phenomenology, psychological science and common sense. In G.R. Semin & K.J. Gergen (Eds.) *Everyday understanding: Social and scientific implications*. London: Sage, 64-82.

Giorgi, A. (1999). A phenomenological perspective on some phenomenographic results on learning. *Journal on Phenomenological Psychology* 30 (2), 68-94.

Giorgi, A. (2002). The question of validity in qualitative research. *Journal of Phenomenological Psychology* 33 (1), 1-18.

Giorgi, A. (2005). The phenomenological movement and research in the human sciences. *Nursing Science Quarterly* 18 (1), 75-82.

Glaser, B. & Strauss, A. (1967). *The discovery of grounded theory: Strategies for qualitative research*. Chicago, IL: Aldine.

Greenfield, S. (1999). Soul, brain and mind. In J. Crappe (Ed.) *From soul to self.* London: RoutledgeFalmer, 108-125.

Guba, E.G., & Lincoln, Y. S. (1994). Competing paradigms in qualitative research. In N.K. Denzin & Y.S. Lincoln (Eds.) *Handbook of qualitative research*. Thousand Oaks, CA: Sage, 105–117.

Gurwitsch, A. (1964). *The field of consciousness*. (1st ed.). Pittsburg: Duquesne University Press.

Gurwitsch, A. (1966). *Studies in phenomenology and psychology*. Evanston, IL: Northwestern University Press.

Gurwitsch, A. (1982). *The field of consciousness*. (4th ed.). Pittsburg: Duquesne University Press.

Haggis, T. (2003). Constructing images of ourselves? A critical investigation into approaches to learning research in higher education. *British Journal of Educational Research* 29 (1), 89–104

Hales, R. & Watkins, M. (2004). The potential contribution of phenomenography to study individuals' meanings of environmental responsibility. Paper presented at International Outdoor Education Research Conference La Trobe University Bendigo, Victoria, Australia. July 2004. <http://www.latrobe.edu.au/oent/OE_conference_2004/papers/hales.pdf>. Accessed 27th May 2006.

Hasselgren, B. & Beach, D. (1997). Phenomenography – a "good-for-nothing brother" of phenomenology? *Higher Education Research and Development 16* (2), 191-202.

Hasselgren, B., & Beach, D. (1998). Phenomenography – a "good-for-nothing brother" of phenomenology? Report from Department of Education and Educational Research, Göteborg University.

Heath, H. & Cowley, S. (2004). Developing grounded theory approach: a comparison of Glaser and Strauss. *International Journal of Nursing Studies* 41, 141-150.

Husén, T. (1997). Research paradigms in education. In J.P. Keeves (Ed.) *Educational research methodology and measurement: an international handbook*. Oxford: Pergamon, 16-21.

Husserl, E. (1973). *Experience and judgement*. Evanston, IL: Northwestern University Press.

Huusko, M. & Paloniemi, S. (2006). Fenomenografia laadullisena tutkimussuuntauksena kasvatustieteissä. *Kasvatus* 37 (2), 162-173.

Illeris, K. (2002). *The three dimensions of learning*. Frederiksberg: Roskilde University Press.

Jarvis, P. (2004) *Adult and continuing education: Theory and practice*. (3rd ed.). London: RoutledgeFalmer.

Johansson, B., Marton, F. & Svensson, L. (1985). An approach to describing learning as a change between qualitatively different conceptions. In A.L. Pines & T.H. West (Eds.) *Cognitive structure and conceptual change*. New York: Academic Press, 233-257.
Jokinen, A. & Juhila, K. (1991). Diskursseja rakentamassa. Näkökulmia sosiaalisten käytäntöjen tutkimiseen. Tampereen yliopisto. Sosiaalipolitiikan laitos. Tutkimuksia sarja A 2.
Järvenoja, H. & Järvelä, S. (2005). How students describe the sources of their emotional and motivational experiences during the learning process: A qualitative approach. *Learning and Instruction* 15, 465-480.
Järvinen, P. & Järvinen, A. (2000). *Tutkimustyön metodeista*. Tampere: Opinpajan kirja.
Kaila, E. cited in Rauhala, L. (1998). *Ihmisen ainutlaatuisuus*. Helsinki: University Press.
Karvonen, E. 1997. Kohti relationaalista tietokäsitystä. In K. Stachon (Ed.) *Näkökulmia tietoyhteiskuntaan*. Helsinki: Gaudeamus, 171-204.
Kelly, P. (2002). *Validity and discursive phenomenography*. Paper presented at the Annual Conference of the British Educational Research Association. September 2002. University of Exeter, England. <http://www.leeds.ac.uk/educol/documents/00003084.htm>. Accessed 30th March 2004.
Kerlinger, F. (1973). *Foundations of behavioural research*. New York: Holt, Rinehart & Winston.
Ki, W.W., Lam, H.C., Chung, A.L.S., Tse, S.K., Ko, P.Y., Lau, E.C.C., Chou, W.Y., Lai, A.C.Y. & Lai, S.M.S. (2003). Structural awareness, variation theory and ICT support. *L1 - Educational Studies in Language and Literature* 3, 53-78.
Kirk, J. (2002). *Theorising information use*. Doctoral thesis. University of Technology. Sidney, Australia.
Kroksmark, T. (1987). *Fenomenografisk didaktik*. Göteborg: Acta Universitatis Gothoburgensis.
Kroksmark, T. (2006 in print). *@orgraphy. Some aspects on the digital life-world*. <http://www.hlk.hj.se/upload_dir/517014e21633c6de1093ca92e7b0a777.pdf>. Accessed 7th May 2006.
Kvale, S. (1989). To validate is to question. In S. Kvale (Ed.) *Issues of validity in qualitative research*. Lund: Studentlitteratur, 73-92.
Kvale, S. (1995). The social construction of validity. *Qualitative Inquiry* 1 (1), 19-40.
Kvale, S. (1996). *InterViews: An introduction to qualitative research interviewing*. Thousand Oaks, CA: Sage.
Larsson, S. (1998). *On quality in qualitative studies*. Contribution to the 1st international workshop: biographical research in social and educational sciences. Revised version of a paper presented at the ECER-conference in Ljubljana.
<http://www.leeds.ac.uk/educol/documents/000000821.htm>. Accessed 18th August 2004.
Lather, P. (1993). Fertile obsession: validity after poststructuralism. *Sosiological Quarterly* 4, (673-693).
Lather, P. (1995). The validity of angels: Interpretive and textual strategies in researching the lives of women with HIV/ADS. *Qualitative Inquiry* 1, 41-61.
Latomaa, T. (2005). Ymmärtävä psykologia: psykologia rekonstruktiivisena tieteenä. In J. Perttula & T. Latomaa (Eds.) Kokemuksen tutkimus. Merkitys – tulkinta – ymmärtäminen. Helsinki: Dialogia, 17-88.
Laurillard, D. (1993). *Rethinking university teaching*. London: RoutledgeFalmer.
Lave, J. (1996). Teaching, as learning, in practice. *Mind, Culture and Activity*, 3 (3), 149-163.
Lawler, P.A. & King, K.P. (2003). Changes, challenges and future. *New Directions for Adult and Continuing Education* 98, 83-91.

Leinhardt, G., McCarthy Young, K. & Merriman, J. (1995). Integrating professional knowledge: The theory of practice and the practice of theory. *Learning and Instruction* 5, 401-408.
Limberg, L. (1999). Experiencing information seeking and learning: a study of the interaction between two phenomena. *Information Research* 5 (1). <http://InformationR.net/ir/5-1/paper68.html>. Accessed 4th April 2006.
Linder, C. & Marshall, D. (2003). Reflection and phenomenography: towards theoretical and educational development possibilities. *Learning and Instruction* 13 (3), 271- 284.
Luque, L.M. (2003). The role of domain-specific knowledge in intentional conceptional change. In G.M. Sinatra and P.R. Pintrich (Eds.) *Intentional conceptional change*. Mahwah, NJ: Lawrence Erlbaum Associates, 133-170.
Luomanen, J., & Räsänen, P. (2002). *Tietokoneavusteinen laadullinen analyysi ja QSR NVivo-ohjelmisto*. Turun yliopisto, sosiologian laitos. Sosiologian tutkimuksia. Digipaino.
Lycan, W.G. (1996). *Consciousness and experience*. Massachusetts: The MIT Press.
Malterud, K. (2001). Qualitative research: standards, challenges, and guidelines. *Lancet* 8 (11), 483-488.
Marton, F. (1974). *Inlärning och studiefärdighet*. Rapporter från Pedagogiska Institutionen, nr 121. Göteborgs Universitet.
Marton, F. (1978). *Describing conceptions of the world around us*. Reports from the Institute of Education, nro 66. University of Göteborg.
Marton, F. (1981). Phenomenography – describing conceptions of the world around us. *Instructional Science* 10, 177-200.
Marton, F. (1986). Phenomenography: a research approach to investigating different understandings of reality. *Journal of Thought* 21 (3), 28-49.
Marton, F. (1988). Phenomenography: exploring different conceptions of reality. In D.M. Fetterman (Ed.) *Qualitative approaches to evaluation in education: the silent revolution*. New York: Praeger, 176 - 205.
Marton, F. (1992). *Notes on ontology*. Unpublished manuscript. Cited in M. Uljens (1996). On the philosophical foundation of phenomenography. In G. Dall'Alba & B. Hasselgren (Eds.) *Reflections on phenomenography – Toward a methodology?* Göteborg Studies in educational sciences 109. Acta Universitatis Gothoburgensis, 103-128.
Marton, F. (1994a). Phenomenography. In T. Husén & T.N. Postlethwaite (Eds.) *The international encyclopedia of education*, vol 8. Oxford: Pergamon, 4424-4429. <http://www.ped.gu.se/biorn/phgraph/civil/main/1res.appr.html>. Accessed 24th March 2003.
Marton, F. (1994b). On the structure of teachers' awareness. In I. Carlgren, G. Handal & S. Vaage (Eds.) *Teachers' minds and actions*. London: The Falmer Press, 28 - 42.
Marton, F. (1996a). Cognoso ergo sum – Reflections on reflections. In G. Dall'Alba & B. Hasselgren (Eds.) *Reflections on phenomenography. Toward a methodology?* Göteborg Studies in Educational Sciences 109, Acta Universitatis Gothoburgensis, 163-187.
Marton, F. (1996b). *Is phenomenography phenomenology?* <http://www.ped.gu.se/biorn/phgraph/civil/faq/faq.phen.html>. Accessed 24th March 2003.
Marton, F. (1997). Phenomenography. In J.P. Keeves (Ed.) *Educational research, methodology, and measurement: an international handbook*. (2nd ed.). Oxford: Pergamon, 95-101.
Marton, F. (2000). The structure of awareness. In Bowden, J. and Walsh, E (Eds.) *Phenomenography*. Melbourne: RMIT University Press, 102-116.
Marton, F., & Booth, S. (1997). *Learning and awareness*. Mahwah, NJ: Lawrence Erlbaum Associates.
Marton, F. & Booth, S. (1998). The learner's experience of learning. In D.R. Olson & N.

Torrance (Eds.) *The handbook of education and human development. New models of learning, teaching and schooling.* Oxford: Blackwell Publishers, 534-564.

Marton, F. & Fai, P.M. (1999). *Two faces of variation.* Paper presented at 8th European Conference for Learning and Instruction. August 1999. Göteborg, Sweden.

Marton, F. & Pong, W.Y. (2005). On the unit of description in phenomenography. *Higher Education Research & Development* 24 (4), 335-348.

Marton, F. & Trigwell, K. (2000). Variatio est mater studiorum. *Higher Education Research & Development* 19 (3), 381- 395.

Marton, F. & Tsui, A.B.M. (2004). *Classroom discourse and the space of learning.* Mahwah, NJ: Lawrence Erlbaum Associates.

Marton, F., Beaty, E., & Dall'Alba, G. (1993). Conceptions of learning. *International Journal of Educational Research* 19, 277–300.

Marton, F., Runesson, U. & Tsui, A.B.M. (2004). The space of learning. In F. Marton & A.B.M. Tsui (Eds.) *Classroom discourse and the space of learning.* Mahwah, NJ: Lawrence Erlbaum Associates, 3-40.

Marton, F., Watkins, D. & Tang, C. (1997). Discontinuities and continuities in the experience of learning: an interview study of high-school students in Hong Kong. *Learning and Instruction* 7 (1), 21-48.

Matthews, M.R. (1997). Introductory comments on philosophy and constructivism in science education. *Science & Education* 6, 5-14.

McCann, E.J. & Carcia, T. (1999). Maintaining motivation and regulating emotion: Measuring individual differences in academic volitional strategies. *Learning and Individual Differences* 11 (3), 259-279.

McKenzie, J.A. (2003). *Variation and change in university teachers' ways of experiencing teaching.* Doctoral thesis. University of Technology, Sidney, Australia.

Mead, G.H. (1934). *Mind, self and society.* Chicago, IL: Chicago University Press.

Merriam, S. (1988). *Case study research in education.* San Francisco: Jossey Bass.

Mezirow, J. (1996). Toward a learning theory of adult literacy. *Adult Basic Education* 6 (3), 115-126.

Mezirow, J. (2000). Learning to think like an adult. Core conceptions of transformation theory. In J. Mezirow and Associates. *Learning as transformation. Critical perspectives on a theory in progress.* San Francisco, CA: Jossey-Bass, 3-33.

Moilanen, P. (2000). Interpretation, truth and correspondence. *Journal of the Theory of Social Behaviour* 30 (4), 377-390.

Moustakas, C. (1994). *Phenomenological research methods.* Thousand Oaks, CA: Sage.

Niemi, H. (2002). Empowering learners in the virtual university. In H. Niemi and P. Ruohotie (Eds.) *Theoretical understanding for learning in the virtual university.* Hämeenlinna: Research Centre for Vocational Education, University of Tampere, 1-35.

Niikko, A. (2003). *Fenomenografia kasvatustieteellisessä tutkimuksessa.* (Phenomenographic in educational research). University of Joensuu, Research Reports of the Faculty of Education. No 85.

Niiniluoto, I & Saarinen, E. (Eds.) (2002). *Nykyajan filosofia.* Juva: WS Bookwell Oy.

Niiniluoto, I. (1983). *Tieteellinen päättely ja selittäminen.* Helsinki: Otava.

Olesen, H.S. (1996). *Adult education and everyday life.* Roskilde: Roskilde University Centre.

Oosterheert, I.E. & Vermunt, J.D. (2001). Individual differences in learning to teach: Relating cognition, regulation and affect. *Learning and Instruction* 11 (2), 133–156.

Pang, M.F. (2003). Two faces of variation: On continuity in the phenomenographic movement. *Scandinavian Journal of Educational research* 47 (2), 145 – 156.

Patton, M. (2002). *Qualitative research & evaluation methods.* (3rd ed.). Thousand Oaks, CA: Sage.
Perttula, J. (1995). *Kokemus psykologisena tutkimuskohteena. Johdatus fenomenologiseen psykologiaan.* Tampere: SUFI.
Phillips, D.C. (1995). The good, the bad, and the ugly: The many faces of constructivism. *Educational Research* 24, 5-12.
Phillips, V. & Bond, C. (2004). Undergraduates' experiences of critical thinking. *Higher Education Research & Development* 23 (3), 277-294.
Piaget, J. (1983). Piaget's theory. In P. H. Mussen (Ed.) *Handbook of child psychology.* New York: Wiley, 103–128.
Pintrich, P.R. (2000a). The role of motivation in self-regulated learning. In P.R. Pintrich & P. Ruohotie (Eds.) *Conative constructs and self-regulated learning.* Hämeenlinna: Research Centre for Vocational Education, University of Tampere, 51-66.
Pintrich, P. R. (2000b). The role of goal orientation in self-regulated learning. In M. Boekaerts, P. R. Pintrich, & M. Zeidner (Eds.) *Handbook of self-regulation.* San Diego: Academic Press, 451–502.
Pohland, P. & Bova, B. (2000). Professional development as transformational learning. *International Journal of Leadership in Education* 3 (2), 137-150.
Pong, W.Y. (1999). *The dynamics of awareness.* Paper presented at the 8th EARLI conference. August 1999. Göteborg, Sweden.
Ponterotto, J.G. (2005). Qualitative research in counseling psychology: A primer on research paradigms and philosophy of science. *Journal on Counseling Psychology* 52 (2), 126-136.
Pring, R. (2005). *Philosophy of education. aims, theory, common sense and research.* London: Continuum.
Pritchard, T., Heatly, R. & Trigwell, K. (2005). How art, media and design students conceive of the relation between the dissertation and practice. *Art, Design & Communication in Higher Education* 4 (1), 5-15.
Prosser, M. (2005). Conceptions of subject matter, research and approach to teaching. Paper presented at British Journal of Educational Psychology Conference 2005. May 2005. University of Edinburgh, Edinburgh, Scotland.
Prosser, M., Martin, E., Triggwell, K., Ramsden, P. & Lueckenhausen, G. (2005). Academic's experiences of understanding of their subject matter and relationship of this to their experiences of teaching and learning. *Instructional Science* 33, 137-157.
Prosser, M., & Trigwell, K. (1999). *Understanding learning and teaching: The experience in higher education.* Buckingham: Open University Press.
Prosser, M., Trigwell, K. & Taylor, P. (1994). A phenomenographic study of academics' conceptions of science learning and teaching. *Learning and Instruction* 4 (3), 217-231.
Puolimatka, T. (2002a). *Opetuksen teoria. Konstruktivismista realismiin.* Helsinki: Tammi.
Puolimatka, T. (2002b). Kvalitatiivisen tutkimuksen luotettavuus ja totuusteoriat. *Kasvatus* 33 (5), 466-474.
Ramsden, P., Masters, G., Stephanou, A., Walsh, E., Martin, E., Laurillard, D., & Marton, F. (1993). Phenomenographic research and the measurement of understanding: an investigation of students' conceptions of speed, distance, and time. *International Journal of Educational Research* 19 (3), 301-316.
Rauhala, L. (1981). *Merkityksen ongelma psykologiassa ja psykiatriassa.* Helsingin yliopiston psykologian laitoksen soveltavan psykologian osaston tutkimuksia 8. Helsingin yliopisto.
Rauhala, L. (1989). *Ihmisen ykseys ja moninaisuus.* Helsinki: Sairaanhoitajien koulutussäätiö.
Rauhala, L. (1992). *Humanistinen psykologia.* Helsinki: Yliopistopaino.

Rauhala, L. (1993). *Eksistentiaalinen fenomenologia hermeneuttisen tieteenfilosofian menetelmänä. Maailmankuvan kokonaisrakenteen erittelyä ihmistä koskevien tieteiden kysymyksissä.* Filosofisia tutkimuksia Tampereen yliopistosta, Vol. 41, SUFI 8.
Rauhala, L. (1995). *Tajunnan itsepuolustus.* Helsinki: Yliopistopaino.
Rauhala, L. (1996). Tajunnan itsepuolustus. *Tiedepolitiikka* 1/96, 35-42.
Rauhala, L. (1997). Tajunnan tutkimus sen oman struktuurin ehdoilla. *niin& näin. Filosofinen aikakauslehti* 1/97, 64-68. http://www.netn.fi/197/netn_197_rauha.html. Accessed 22nd January 2004.
Rauhala, L. (1998). *Ihmisen ainutlaatuisuus.* Helsinki: University Press.
Rauhala, L. (2002). Subjektiivisen maailmankuvan muutos oppimisessa ja kasvatuksessa. Aivot, maailmankuva, informaatiotulva – opettajuus? Artikkelisarja. *OKKA-säätiön vuosikirja 2002*, 33-41.
Richardson, J.T.E. (1999). The concepts and methods of phenomenographic research. *Review of Educational Research* 69 (1), 53-82.
Richardson, L. (1995). Poetics, dramatics, and transgressive validity: The case of skipped line. *Sociological Quarterly* 4, 695-710.
Runesson, U. (1999). *Teaching as constituting a space of variation.* Paper presented at the 8th European Conference for Learning and Instruction. August 1999. Göteborg, Sweden.
Runesson, U. (2006). What is possible to learn? On variation as a necessary condition for learning. *Scandinavian Journal of Educational Research* 50 (4), 397-410.
Runesson, U. & Marton, M. (2000). The space of learning. Draftversion, May 2000. To appear in F. Marton & A.B. M. Tsui (Eds.) *Classroom discourse and the space of learning.* Mahwah, NJ: Lawrence Erlbaum Associates.
Runesson, U. & Mok, A.C. (2004). Discernment and the question, "What can be learned?" In F. Marton & A.B.M. Tsui (Eds.) *Classroom discourse and the space of learning.* Mahwah, NJ: Lawrence Erlbaum Associates, 63-87.
Ruohotie, P. (1999). Growth prerequisites in organizations. In P. Ruohotie, H. Tirri, P. Nokelainen & T. Silander. (Eds.) *Modern modelling and professional growth* vol.1. Hämeenlinna: Research Centre for Vocational Education, 5-36.
Ruohotie, P. (2005a). Metakognitiiviset taidot ja käsitteellinen oppiminen. *Ammattikasvatuksen aikakauslehti* 1, 4-11.
Ruohotie, P. (2000b). Conative constructs in learning. In P.R. Pintrich and P. Ruohotie (Eds.) *Conative constructs and self-regulated learning.* Hämeenlinna, Finland: Research Centre for Vocational Education, University of Tampere, 1-30.
Saarinen, E. (1994). *Filosofia.* Porvoo: WSOY.
Sandberg, J. (1994). *Human competence at work: An interpretative perspective.* Doctoral thesis. University of Gothenburg.
Sandberg, J. (1996). Are phenomenographic results reliable? In G. Dall'Alba & B. Hasselgren (Eds.) *Reflections on phenomenography. Toward a methodology?* Göteborg Studies in Educational Sciences 109, Acta Universitatis Gothoburgensis, 129-140.
Sandberg, J. (1997). Are phenomenographic results reliable? *Higher Education Research & Development* 16 (2), 203 -212.
Sandberg, J. (2005). How do we justify knowledge produced within interpretative approaches? *Organizational Research Methods* 8 (1), 41-68.
Schunk, D.H. (2005). Commentary on self-regulation in school contexts. *Learning and Instruction* 15, 173-177.
Schön, D.A. (1987). *Educating the reflective practitioner.* San Francisco: Jossey-Bass.

Sinatra, G.M. & Pintrich, P.R. (2003). The role of intentions in conceptual change learning. In G.M. Sinatra and P.R. Pintrich (Eds.) *Intentional conceptional change*. Mahwah, NJ: Lawrence Erlbaum Associates, 1-18.

Sjöström, B. & Dahlgren L.O. (2002). Nursing theory and concept development or analysis. Applying phenomenography in nursing research. *Journal of Advanced Nursing* 40 (3), 339-345.

Sonnemann, U. (1954) *Existence and Therapy: An Introduction to Phenomenological Psychology and Existential Analysis*. New York: Grune & Stratton.

Souvignier, E. & Mokhlesgerami, J. (2006). Using self-regulation as a framework for implementing strategy instruction to foster reading comprehension. *Learning and Instruction* 16, 57-71.

Strauss, A & Corbin, J. (1994). Grounded theory methodology: An overview. In N.K. Denzin & Y.S. Lincoln (Eds.) *Handbook of qualitative research*. (1st ed.). Thousand Oaks, CA: Sage, 273-285.

Svensson, L. (1976). *Study skill and learning*. Göteborg: Acta Universitatis Gothoburgensis.

Svensson, L. (1994) Theoretical foundations of Phenomenography. In R. Ballantyne & C. Bruce (Eds.) *Phenomenography: Philosophy and Practice*. Proceedings. Queensland University of Technology, Brisbane Australia, 9-20.

Svensson, L. (1997). Theoretical foundations of phenomenography. *Higher Education Research & Development* 16 (2), 159 – 171.

Svensson. L. & Theman, J. (1983). *The relation between categories of description and an interview protocol in a case of phenomenographic research*. Paper presented at the Second Annual Human Science Research Conference, Duquesne University, May 1983, Pittsburg, P.A. USA, [Report from the Institute of Education, Göteborg University, No. 1983:02

Säljö, R. (1975). *Qualitative differences in learning as a function of the learner's conception of the task*. Göteborg: Acta Universitatis Gothoburgensis.

Säljö, R. (1979). *Learning in the learner's perspective: 1, Some common-sense conceptions*. University of Göteborg, Department of Education Report No. 76.

Säljö, R. (1982). *Learning and understanding: A study of differences in constructing meaning from a text*. Göteborg: Acta Universitatis Gothoburgensis.

Säljö, R. (1988). Learning in educational settings: Methods of inquiry. In P. Ramsden (Ed.) *Improving learning: New perspectives*. London: Kogan Page, 32-48.

Säljö, R. (1996). Minding action – Conceiving of the world versus participating in cultural practices. In G. Dall'Alba & B. Hasselgren (Eds.) *Reflections on phenomenography. Toward a methodology?* Göteborg Studies in Educational Sciences 109, Acta Universitatis Gothoburgensis, 19-33.

Säljö, R. (1997). Talk as data and practice – a critical look at phenomenographic inquiry and the appeal to experience. *Higher Education Research & Development* 16 (2), 173 – 190.

Tao, P-K. (2002). A study of students' focal awareness when studying science stories designed for fostering understanding of nature of science. *Research in Science Education* 32, 97-120.

Taylor, S.J. & Bodgan, R. (1984). *Introduction to qualitative research methods – The search for meaning*. New York: John Wiley and Sons.

Theman, J. (1983). *Uppfattningar av politisk makt* [Conceptions of political power]. Göteborg: Acta Universitatis Gothoburgensis.

Trigwell, K. (2000). Phenomenography: Variation and Discernment. In C. Rust (ed.) *Improving student learning*. Proceedings of the 1999 7th International Symposium, Oxford Centre for Staff and Learning Development, Oxford, 75-85.

Trigwell, K. & Prosser, M. 1996. Towards an understanding of individual acts of teaching. Different approaches: Theory and practice in higher education. Proceedings HERDSA Conference. July 1996, Perth, Western Australia. <http://www.herdsa.org.au/confs/1996/trigwell1.html>. Accessed 19th February 2004.

Turunen, K.E. (1998). *Minusta näyttää – Johdatus reflektiiviseen filosofiaan.* Jyväskylä: Atena Kustannus Oy.

Tynjälä, P. (1997). Developing education students' conceptions of the learning process in different learning environments. *Learning and Instruction* 7 (3), 277 – 292.

Tynjälä, P. (1999a). *Oppiminen tiedon rakentamisena. Konstruktivistisen oppimiskäsityksen perusteita.* Helsinki: Kirjayhtymä.

Tynjälä, P. (1999b). Towards expert knowledge? A comparison between a constructivist and traditional learning environment in the university. *International Journal of Educational Research* 31 (5), 357 – 442.

Uljens, M. (1996). On the philosophical foundation of phenomenography. In G. Dall'Alba & B. Hasselgren (Eds.) *Reflections on phenomenography – Toward a methodology?* Göteborg Studies in educational sciences 109. Acta Universitatis Gothoburgensis, 103 – 128.

Uljens, M. (1997). *School didactics and learning: a school didactic model framing an analysis of pedagogical implications of learning theory.* Hove: Psychology Press.

Usher, E.L. & Pajares, F. (2006). Sources of academic and self-regulatory efficacy beliefs of entering middle school students. *Contemporary Educational Psychology* 31, 125-141.

Van Eekelen, I.M., Boshuizen, H.P.A. & Vermunt, J.D. (2005). Self-regulation in higher education teacher learning. *Higher Education* 50, 447–471.

Van Eekelen, I.M., Vermunt, J.D. & Boshuizen, H.P.A. (in press). Exploring teachers' will to learn. *Teaching and Teacher Education.*

Van Manen, M. (1990). *Researching lived experience: human science for an action sensitive pedagogy.* New York: State University of New York Press.

Watkins, M. (2000). Ways of learning about leisure meanings. *Leisure Science* 22, 93-107.

Vermunt, J.D. (1996). Metacognitive, cognitive and affective aspects of learning styles and strategies. A phenomenographic analysis. *Higher Education* 31, 25 – 50.

Vermunt, J.D. (1998). The regulation of constructive learning processes. *British Journal of Educational Psychology* 68, 149–171.

Wertheimer, M. (1945). *Productive thinking.* New York: Harper.

Wihlborg, M. (year unknown). *Using a poststructural critical lens to looking through the humanist facade, in order to make the gender aspect visible in phenomenographic research about learning and meaning (in a broad sense).* <http://k1.ioe.ac.uk/pesgb/z/Wihlborg.pdf>. Accessed 15th March 2005.

Von Glasersfeld, E. (1995). A constructivist approach to teaching. In L. P. Steffe & T. Wood (Eds.) *Constructivism in education* Hillsdale, NJ: Lawrence Erlbaum Associates, 3–16.

Wood, K. (2000). The experience of learning to teach: changing student teachers' way of understanding teaching. *Journal of Curriculum Studies* 32 (1), 75-93.

Wood, K. (2006). Changing as a person: the experience of learning to research in the social sciences. *Higher Education Research & Development* 25 (1), 53–66.

Vosniadou, S. (1994). Capturing and modelling the process of conceptual change. *Learning and Instruction* 4, 45-69.

Vosniadou, S. & Verschaffel, L. (2004). The Problem of Conceptual Change in Mathematics. In L.Verschaffel & S. Vosniadou (Eds.) Conceptual Change in Mathematics Learning and Teaching, *Special Issue of Learning and Instruction* 14, 445-451.

Vygotsky, L. (1978). *Mind in society: The development of higher psychological processes.*

Cambridge, MA: Harvard University Press.
Zimmerman, B.J. (2002). Becoming a self-regulated learner: an overview. *Theory into Practice* 21 (2), 64–70.
Zimmerman, B.J. and Schunk, D.H. (2001). *Self-regulated learning and academic achievement; theoretical perspectives.* Mahwah, NJ: Lawrence Erlbaum Associates.
Åkerlind, G. S. (1999). *Growing and developing as an academic: what does it mean?* Paper presented at HERDSA Annual International Conference, July 1999. Melbourne, Australia.
Åkerlind, G. S. (2002a). *Academics' awareness of their own growth and development – five dimensions of variation.* Paper presented at the Symposium "Current issues in phenomenography". November 2002. Canberra, Australia.
Åkerlind, G. S. (2002b). *Principles and practice in phenomenographic research.* Paper presented at the Symposium "Current issues in phenomenography". November 2002. Canberra, Australia.
Åkerlind, G. S. (2005a). Variation and commonality in phenomenographic research methods. *Higher Education Research & Development*, 24 (4), 321-334.
Åkerlind, G. S. (2005b). Academic growth and development – How do university academics experience it? *Higher Education*, 50, 1-32.
Åkerlind, G. S., Bowden, J., & Green, P. (in press). Learning to do phenomenography: A reflective discussion. In J. Bowden & P. Green (Eds.) *Doing phenomenography.* Melbourne: RMIT University Press.

Unpublished references

Educational Resources Information Centre (ERIC), Definition of the term professional development.
<http://eric.ed.gov/ERICWebPortal/Home.portal?_nfpb=true&portlet_thesaurus >. Accessed 2nd March 2006.
Kyrö, P. Dynamics of Learning in Transitions — DYLETRA
<http://www.uta.fi/eduta/dyletra/dyletra/01dyletra1aims.html>. Accessed 22nd July 2005.
Nieminen, J. (2005). TUKEVA PowerPoint presentation.

Wissenschaftlicher Buchverlag bietet

kostenfreie

Publikation

von

wissenschaftlichen Arbeiten

Diplomarbeiten, Magisterarbeiten, Master und Bachelor Theses
sowie Dissertationen, Habilitationen und wissenschaftliche Monographien

Sie verfügen über eine wissenschaftliche Abschlußarbeit zu aktuellen oder zeitlosen Fragestellungen, die hohen inhaltlichen und formalen Ansprüchen genügt, und haben **Interesse an einer honorarvergüteten Publikation**?

Dann senden Sie bitte erste Informationen über Ihre Arbeit per Email an info@vdm-verlag.de. Unser Außenlektorat meldet sich umgehend bei Ihnen.

VDM Verlag Dr. Müller Aktiengesellschaft & Co. KG
Dudweiler Landstraße 125a
D - 66123 Saarbrücken

www.vdm-verlag.de

Made in the USA
Lexington, KY
19 March 2013